Reading for Every Child
Vocabulary

Grade 4

by
Robyn Raymer

Published by Instructional Fair
an imprint of
Frank Schaffer Publications®

Instructional Fair

Author: Robyn Raymer
Editor: Linda Triemstra
Interior Designer: Lori Kibbey

Frank Schaffer Publications®

Instructional Fair is an imprint of Frank Schaffer Publications.

Send all inquiries to:
Frank Schaffer Publications
3195 Wilson Drive NW
Grand Rapids, Michigan 49534

Reading for Every Child: Vocabulary—grade 4

ISBN: 0-7424-2844-3

2 3 4 5 6 7 8 9 10 PAT 10 09 08 07

 **Vocabulary**

Table of Contents

Reading First 4

Introduction **5**

Our Five Senses...6

Dressing Up 9

People You Meet 12

Right on Time! 15

What Does That Stand For? 18

High Tech 21

Can You Hear Me? 24

Tusks, Talons, and Tentacles 27

Let's Get Wet!...30

Homophones 33

Review **36**

Don't Be So Unfriendly!..40

The World Around Us 43

Good Night, Sleep Tight! 46

How Do You Feel About Synonyms? 49

Just the Opposite...52

At the Doctor's Office 55

Word Families 58

English Words from French and Spanish 61

Moving Around 64

Word Roots 67

Review **70**

Teacher Resources **73**

Answer Key **79**

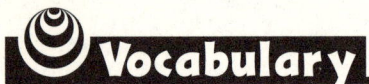

Reading First

The Reading First program is part of the No Child Left Behind Act. This program is based on research by the National Reading Panel that identifies five key areas for early reading instruction—phonemic awareness, phonics, fluency, vocabulary, and comprehension.

Phonemic Awareness

Phonemic awareness focuses on a child's understanding of letter sounds and the ability to manipulate those sounds. Listening is a crucial component, as the emphasis at this level is on sounds that are heard and differentiated in each word the child hears.

Phonics

After students recognize sounds that make up words, they must then connect those sounds to *written* text. An important part of phonics instruction is systematic encounters with letters and letter combinations.

Fluency

Fluent readers are able to recognize words quickly. They are able to read aloud with expression and do not stumble over words. The goal of fluency is to read more smoothly and with *comprehension*.

Vocabulary

In order to understand what they read, students must first have a solid base of vocabulary words. As students increase their vocabulary knowledge, they also increase their comprehension and fluency.

Comprehension

Comprehension is "putting it all together" to understand what has been read. With fiction and nonfiction texts, students become active readers as they learn to use specific comprehension strategies before, during, and after reading.

Introduction

Reading/language arts specialists agree that students need direct vocabulary instruction such as the lessons in *Reading for Every Child: Vocabulary.* Vocabulary teaching is essential because children cannot comprehend what they read unless they understand most of the words in their reading materials. Although students learn word meanings indirectly through conversation, reading, and even watching movies and television shows, direct instruction bolsters and enriches their understanding, making them stronger readers and fluent, confident speakers and writers.

Students usually have little difficulty mastering new or semi-familiar words that name or describe well-known objects and concepts. Word Banks in the first half of *Reading for Every Child: Vocabulary* consist of words like these (e.g., *astronaut* or *sleeve*). Learning unfamiliar words for unknown objects and concepts presents the greatest challenge. That is why this book teaches such words in the last few lessons (examples are *intestines* and *nightingale*).

The Word Banks in the book are seven to nine words long. They are grouped by theme or word type. For example, What Does That Stand For? explores acronyms such as *A.M., P.M.,* and *CD*. English Words from French and Spanish teaches words such as *banquet, boulevard, canyon,* and *patio*. Each lesson contains a majority of easier, more familiar words and two to three that present more of a challenge.

Suggestions for Classroom Use

Since students' thinking, reading, and writing skills vary, you may need to modify the activities and suggestions below to fit your students' individual needs. For example, you might reproduce some pages as overhead transparencies and complete them as a class.

Getting to Know New Words: This section presents a strong context sentence for each word in the Word Bank. By choosing from among four possible ways to restate a word, or a phrase containing a word, students learn or confirm its definition. If a word has two commonly used meanings, for example, *a lace veil* and *a shoelace*, it appears in two context sentences.

Vocabulary Practice and Extra Practice: These sections provide two more opportunities to work with each word in the Word Bank. One section requires writing the words, reinforcing spellings and meanings. Activities in these sections include grouping words with synonyms or related words, identifying synonym, antonym, or homophone pairs, completing sentences that contain list words, and completing charts that group list words according to their meanings. You may wish to have your students complete one or both of these sections, depending on their needs.

Word Play: This enrichment section includes puzzles and riddles, as well as analogies to prepare students for analogy items in standardized tests. Word Play activities are meant to challenge students.

Writing Activities: This section provides opportunities for students to use Word Bank words in a variety of forms, including emails, dialogues, jokes, poems, songs, folktales, advertisements, and phone messages. Note that each writing activity includes an example. These are meant to inspire students to use words in creative ways. If your students tend to copy rather than use examples as jumping-off spots for their ideas, you may wish to have them complete the activities without reading the examples.

Teacher Resource Pages: These pages provide suggestions for basic vocabulary instruction (such as preteaching vocabulary before reading), additional enrichment activities, and a list of books on vocabulary instruction.

Our Five Senses

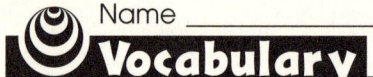

Word Bank			
beige	greenery	hisses	odor
perfumed	rumbled	slick	watermelon

Getting to Know New Words

Directions: Read each sentence. Then choose the best word or phrase to replace the underlined word(s). Circle the letter next to your choice.

1. The fawn has some white markings, but most of its fur looks <u>beige</u>.
   a. warm
   b. black
   c. tan
   d. soft

2. In this hot, dry desert there is not much <u>greenery</u>.
   a. green paint
   b. time for gardening
   c. greenish water
   d. green plant life

3. A cat <u>hisses</u> and shows its teeth when it is angry or scared.
   a. purrs
   b. makes an "aaaarrrr!" sound
   c. mews
   d. makes a "HISSSS!" sound

4. These eggs have a stinky <u>odor</u>, so they must be rotten.
   a. sound
   b. taste
   c. smell
   d. color

5. The roses' sweet smell <u>perfumed the house</u>.
   a. cleaned the house
   b. made the house smell sweet
   c. sprinkled the house with ladies' perfume
   d. sprinkled rose petals around the house

6. All night huge trucks <u>rumbled by</u>, keeping me awake.
   a. rolled noisily by
   b. rode quickly by
   c. let out smoke nearby
   d. streaked past

7. The roads were <u>slick</u> with ice, so Mom drove cautiously.
   a. slippery
   b. dry
   c. crunchy
   d. covered

8. My favorite summer fruit is <u>watermelon</u>.
   a. a small, round, dark-blue berry
   b. a fruit with a pit inside and fuzzy skin
   c. a juicy, red berry with seeds on the outside
   d. a big fruit with a green rind and juicy, red pulp

 **Vocabulary**

Vocabulary Practice

Directions: Write the word from the Word Bank that best completes each group.

1. cantaloupe, honeydew melon, _____

2. trees, plants, bushes, _____

3. smell, scent, aroma, _____

4. freshened, sweetened, scented, _____

5. snake, cat, warning, _____

6. tan, light brown, yellowish, _____

7. boomed, crashed, thundered, _____

8. slippery, icy, muddy, _____

Word Bank			
beige	greenery	hisses	odor
perfumed	rumbled	slick	watermelon

Extra Practice

Directions: Choose the best way to complete each sentence or answer each question. Write the correct letter on the line.

1. What **rumbled** down the mountain? _____   a. a forest

2. What **perfumed** the bedroom? _____   b. the refrigerator

3. What made the floor **slick**? _____   c. mud

4. What uses a horrid **odor** to protect itself? _____   d. a boulder

5. What kind of animal has **beige** fur? _____   e. a deer

6. Where can you go to see lots of **greenery**? _____   f. a skunk

7. **Watermelon** gets chilly if you put it in _____.   g. flowers

8. What **hisses** to warn other creatures? _____   h. a snake

Word Play

Directions: Use the clues to complete the crossword puzzle with words from the Word Bank.

DOWN

1. Tan
4. Frigid
5. Goes "SSSSS!"
7. Scented
10. Smell

ACROSS

2. Thunder did this.
3. A saucy dessert
6. Like wet clay or a banana peel
8. You see it in a plant store.
9. A juicy treat with seeds

Write a Vivid Description

Directions: Choose words from the Word Bank that help you imagine sights, sounds, smells, flavors, and ways that things feel. Write a paragraph that will help readers see, hear, smell, taste, and feel along with you. Use the example to help you.

Word Bank

beige
greenery
hisses
odor
perfumed
rumbled
slick
watermelon
applesauce
chilly

A Summer Day

I'm lying on the front lawn on the hottest day in August. The sprinkler <u>hisses</u> softly. My dog pants in the heat. But what was that other sound? I think my stomach just <u>rumbled</u> with hunger. I go into the house and open the fridge, feeling the <u>chilly</u> air on my sweaty face. Oh, joy! There's a juicy slice of <u>watermelon</u> waiting for me!

Vocabulary
clothing-related nouns; multiple-meaning words

Dressing Up

Word Bank

badge	lace	overalls	scarf
	shabby	sleeve	wreath

Getting to Know New Words

Directions: Read each sentence. Then choose the best word or phrase to replace the underlined word(s). Circle the letter next to your choice.

1. Pinned to the firefighter's uniform was a shiny silver <u>badge</u>.
   a. pin that shows a person has a certain job
   b. silver pin decorated with jewels
   c. necklace or bracelet
   d. pin in the shape of a Dalmatian dog

2. The bride wore a long veil made from white <u>lace</u>.
   a. cloth that has holes as part of its design
   b. thick string
   c. fake fur
   d. cloth printed with a criss-cross pattern

3. When I tried to tie my shoe, the <u>lace</u> broke.
   a. buckle
   b. string
   c. ribbon
   d. Velcro®

4. The farmer pulled on his <u>overalls</u> and fastened the straps.
   a. work shoes
   b. warm shirt
   c. pants with shoulder straps
   d. pants that end at the knee

5. It was windy outside, so Mom tied a <u>scarf</u> over her hair.
   a. straw hat
   b. cloth worn around the head
   c. shower cap
   d. ribbon worn around the waist

6. When I paint, I roll up my right <u>sleeve</u> so it won't get dirty.
   a. shirt pocket
   b. row of buttons
   c. shirt part that circles the neck
   d. shirt part that covers the arm

7. Cinderella's only dress was dirty and <u>shabby</u> from housecleaning.
   a. worn out
   b. tan colored
   c. ruffled
   d. stylish

8. On her head, the bridesmaid wore a pretty <u>wreath</u> of rosebuds.
   a. large number
   b. bouquet
   c. circle
   d. vase

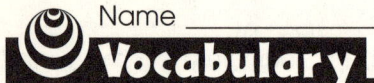
Vocabulary Practice

Directions: Write the word from the Word Bank that best completes each group.

Word Bank
badge
lace
overalls
scarf
shabby
sleeve
wreath

1. cuff, collar, shirt, _____

2. pin, patch, police officer's,_____

3. flowers, circle, Christmas,_____

4. torn, ragged, faded, _____

5. silk, satin, ribbons, _____

6. shorts, pants, jeans, _____

7. necktie, silk, head, _____

Extra Practice

Directions: Choose the best way to answer the question or complete the sentence. Write the correct letter on the line.

1. **Overalls** are pants with shoulder _____.   a. hair

2. Who might wear a **badge**? _____   b. poor

3. Grandma wears a **scarf** to cover her _____.   c. straps

4. People who wear **shabby** clothes may be _____.   d. a bride

5. Ms. Chen hung a holiday **wreath** on her front _____.   e. a guard

6. Your shirt **sleeves** cover your _____.   f. arms

7. Who might wear a **lace** veil? _____   g. door

◎ Vocabulary

Word Play

Word Bank		
badge	scarf	wreath
lace	shabby	cotton
overalls	sleeve	crown

Directions: Write a word from the Word Bank to fit each clue. Find a person who washes clothes without soap or water. **Hint:** Use one list word twice!

1. Officer's pin ___ ___ ___ ___ ___

2. Princess's headgear ___ ___ ___ ___ ___

3. Old and raggedy ___ ___ ___ ___ ___ ___

4. Head or neck cloth ___ ___ ___ ___ ___

5. Shirt part ___ ___ ___ ___ ___ ___

6. Farmer's pants ___ ___ ___ ___ ___ ___ ___ ___

7. Shoestring ___ ___ ___ ___

8. _____ T-shirt ___ ___ ___ ___ ___ ___

9. _____ curtains ___ ___ ___ ___ ___

10. Flower girl's headgear ___ ___ ___ ___ ___ ___

Write About Fancy Clothes

Directions: Pretend you are writing an email to a friend. Use at least three words from the Word Bank to describe what someone wore to a fancy party. You can make your email as silly as you like. Use the example to help you.

Subj: **an outfit that hurt my eyes**
Date: 06/22/2005 9:03:23 AM Mountain Standard Time
From: gossipygail@email.com
To: chattycharlie@email.net

Dear Charlie,

Wow, you should have seen the weird outfit that Julie wore to Shelby's party. You won't believe this: she had on shocking pink overalls over a lime green shirt with puffy sleeves. Her sneakers were neon orange with yellow laces. Her clothes were so bright that they hurt my eyes! Write back soon.

Your friend,
Gail

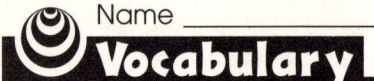 Vocabulary

People You Meet

Word Bank

astronaut	astronomer	newcomer	pupil
relative	veterinarian	volunteer	widow

Getting to Know New Words

Directions: Read each sentence. Then choose the best word or phrase to replace the underlined word(s). Circle the letter next to your choice.

1. The astronaut climbed out of her spacecraft and stepped onto the moon.
   a. scientist
   b. space traveler
   c. alien creature
   d. jet pilot

2. Dr. Stevens is an astronomer who studies stars.
   a. a scientist who studies the universe
   b. a scientist who studies living things
   c. an animal doctor
   d. a children's doctor

3. Danny's family moved often, and he was tired of being a newcomer.
   a. traveler
   b. family member
   c. someone who just left
   d. someone who just arrived

4. When she was in fourth grade, my sister was Ms. McIlvaine's pupil.
   a. student
   b. teacher
   c. principal
   d. daughter

5. Grandma and I look alike, so people can tell she is my relative.
   a. friend
   b. favorite
   c. family member
   d. great-grandmother

6. The veterinarian says our cat needs to lose weight.
   a. animal doctor
   b. pet store owner
   c. retired soldier
   d. children's doctor

7. For two hours a week, Mom works as a volunteer in our school library.
   a. a paid librarian
   b. an unpaid worker
   c. a reading teacher
   d. a writing teacher

8. Grandma has been a widow since Grandpa's death.
   a. stepmother
   b. wife whose husband died
   c. daughter whose dad died
   d. grandmother

 **Vocabulary**

Vocabulary Practice

Directions: Write the word from the Word Bank that best completes each group.

1. student, scholar, learner,

   _____

2. orphan, wife, survivor,

   _____

3. doctor, animals, medicine, _____

4. space shuttle, rocket, traveler, _____

5. stranger, just arrived, _____

6. grandparent, aunt, uncle, _____

7. helper, worker, unpaid, _____

8. scientist, planets, stars, _____

Word Bank

astronaut

astronomer

newcomer

pupil

relative

veterinarian

volunteer

widow

Extra Practice

Directions: Choose the best way to complete each sentence. Write the correct letter on the line.

1. A **veterinarian** helps _____.   a. arrived

2. A **newcomer** is someone who just _____.   b. dead

3. A **relative** is someone in your _____.   c. space

4. A **pupil** learns from her _____.   d. teacher

5. A **widow's** husband is _____.   e. animals

6. An **astronaut** travels in _____.   f. scientist

7. An **astronomer** is a kind of _____.   g. paid

8. **Volunteer** workers are not _____.   h. family

Word Play

Directions: Use the clues to complete the crossword puzzle with words from the Word Bank.

DOWN

1. Uses a sewing machine
3. Cures animals
4. _____ and groom
5. Just got here
8. Spacecraft pilot

ACROSS

2. Family member
6. Her husband died.
7. Space scientist
9. Has a teacher
10. Works for no money

Write a Conversation

Directions: Choose one of these pairs. Write a short conversation they might have. Use the example shown below to help you.

- a tailor and a bride
- a pupil and a newcomer
- an astronaut and an astronomer

Word Bank

astronaut	veterinarian
astronomer	volunteer
newcomer	widow
pupil	bride
relative	tailor

A Conversation Between a Pupil and a Newcomer

"Hi. You just moved here, didn't you?"

"Yeah, my mom's company offered her a better job here, so we had to leave California."

"Really, you used to live in California? Did you see a lot of movie stars there? Did you swim in the ocean all the time?"

"No, I lived in San Francisco. You're thinking of L.A. That's where all the movie stars live. We went to the beach sometimes, but the water was too cold for swimming."

Vocabulary    time-related nouns, verbs, adverbs, and adjectives

Right on Time!

Word Bank			
ancient	annual	briefly	conclude
future	mature	modern	seldom

Getting to Know New Words

Directions: Read each sentence. Then choose the best word or phrase to replace the underlined word(s). Circle the letter next to your choice.

1. <u>Ancient</u> cave paintings show us how humans lived thousands of years ago.
   a. beautiful
   b. very old
   c. detailed
   d. colorful

2. It's time to make plans for our <u>annual</u> Fourth of July picnic.
   a. daily
   b. weekly
   c. monthly
   d. yearly

3. I don't have much time, so I can only <u>explain briefly</u>.
   a. partly explain
   b. explain in a silly way
   c. give a full explanation
   d. take a short time to explain

4. The game will not <u>conclude</u> until one team wins.
   a. get exciting
   b. last
   c. end
   d. begin

5. In <u>the future</u>, people will probably travel to Mars.
   a. the 1980s or 1990s
   b. a month or so
   c. two years
   d. a time that is coming

6. <u>Mature</u> cats are usually not as playful as kittens.
   a. fully grown
   b. adopted
   c. wild
   d. overweight

7. In the past, people died of diseases that <u>modern</u> medicines can cure.
   a. special
   b. tomorrow's
   c. today's
   d. yesterday's

8. My grandparents live so far away that we <u>seldom</u> see them.
   a. usually
   b. are glad to
   c. hardly ever
   d. wish we could

Vocabulary Practice

Directions: Write the word from the Word Bank that best completes each group.

1. end, stop, finalize, _____

2. day, week, month, _____

3. old, elderly, antique,

   _____

4. adult, grown, responsible,

   _____

5. quickly, to make a long story short, _____

6. today's, current, recent, _____

7. tomorrow, later, the year 2020, _____

8. rarely, scarcely, infrequently, _____

Word Bank
ancient

annual

briefly

conclude

future

mature

modern

seldom

Extra Practice

Directions: Choose the best way to complete each sentence. Write the correct letter on the line. **Hint:** Antonyms have opposite meanings.

1. **Conclude** means the opposite of _____.

2. **Seldom** means the opposite of _____.

3. If you speak **briefly** with a friend, your talk is _____.

4. The **future** is anytime after _____.

5. A **mature** animal can have _____.

6. **Modern** is an antonym for _____.

7. **Ancient** is an antonym for _____.

8. An **annual** event happens once _____.

a. a year

b. begin

c. modern

d. short

e. babies

f. today

g. old-fashioned

h. often

Word Play

Directions: Use the clues to solve each riddle with a word from the Word Bank.

Word Bank			
ancient	briefly	future	modern
annual	conclude	mature	seldom

1. Name an antonym for **begin** that ends like **rude**. _____

2. Which word begins like **anniversary** and ends like **usual**? _____

3. Which word begins like **selling** and ends like **kingdom**? _____

4. Which word begins like **modest** and ends like **pattern**? _____

5. Name an antonym for **young** that ends like **efficient**. _____

6. Name an antonym for **past** that ends like **nature**. _____

7. Name an antonym for **slowly** that contains **fly**. _____

8. Name an antonym for **childish** that ends like **sure**. _____

Write a Business Email

Directions: Invent a silly company such as Gum Removers, Inc. or fishfood.com. Use a few words from the Word Bank to write an email to the company president. You can write to complain about something, to ask for a job, or for some other reason. Use the example to help you.

Subj: **My fish won't eat your food!**

Date: 04/07/2005 11:06:27 AM Pacific Standard Time

From: madmaddy@email.net

To: Terry_Tuna@fishfood.com

Dear Mr. Tuna:

In February I bought a box of your Fantastic Fish Food for $5.54, including tax. Well, it's April now, and I have a complaint. Let me explain <u>briefly</u>: your fish food is NOT fantastic. It is not even good. My fish won't eat a bite of it! Before I <u>conclude</u> this email, I wish to demand my money back. I expect you to mail it to me in the VERY near <u>future</u>!

Yours truly,

Madeline Maddox

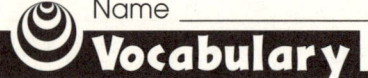
Vocabulary

What Does That Stand For?

Word Bank			
A.M.	CD	P.M.	P.S.
R.S.V.P.	U.S.A.	VCR	www

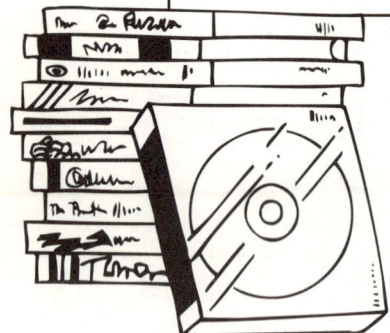

Note on acronyms: Acronyms are letters that stand for words. For example, *TV* stands for *television*. People often use acronyms in place of the words they stand for.

Getting to Know New Words

Directions: Read each sentence. Then choose the best word or phrase to replace the underlined acronym. Circle the letter next to your choice.

1. I usually eat breakfast at 7:30 <u>A.M.</u>
   a. in the summertime
   b. in the evening
   c. in the afternoon
   d. in the morning

2. My favorite singing group has a new <u>CD</u>.
   a. musical disk
   b. software program
   c. movie disk
   d. dance step

3. We usually dine at about 6:30 <u>P.M.</u>
   a. in the springtime
   b. in the evening
   c. in the afternoon
   d. in the morning

4. I forgot to write "Please write back!" in the main part of my letter, so I added it in a <u>P.S.</u>
   a. a part at the beginning
   b. a part at the end
   c. my next letter
   d. a part circled with a heart

5. At the end of his invitation, Pablo wrote <u>R.S.V.P.</u> *555-8534.*
   a. Please phone to tell me if you can come.
   b. Just in case you forgot my phone number...
   c. I really hope you can come.
   d. We changed our phone number to...

6. All fifty states are part of the <u>U.S.A.</u>
   a. Union of Southwest Alabama
   b. Unified States of Asia
   c. United States of America
   d. University of Southern Arizona

7. Please put the videotape in the <u>VCR</u> so we can watch the movie.
   a. machine that shows movies
   b. machine that plays music
   c. store that sells videotapes
   d. store that rents videos

8. Many Web site addresses begin with <u>www</u>.
   a. We will whistle.
   b. Wide, Wonderful World
   c. well, well, well
   d. World Wide Web

Vocabulary

Vocabulary Practice

Directions: Read the hints below. Then match each acronym with the words it stands for. Write the correct letter on the line.

Hints: In Latin, *ante* means "before," *post* means "after," and *meridiem* means "noon." In French, *réspondez, s'il vous plaît* means "please reply." In English, *compact* can mean "small."

1. A.M. _____
2. CD _____
3. P.M. _____
4. P.S. _____
5. R.S.V.P. _____
6. U.S.A. _____
7. VCR _____
8. www _____

a. postscript
b. videocassette recorder
c. World Wide Web
d. compact disk
e. Réspondez, s'il vous plaît
f. post meridiem
g. ante meridiem
h. United States of America

Word Bank
A.M.
CD
P.M.
P.S.
R.S.V.P.
U.S.A.
VCR
www

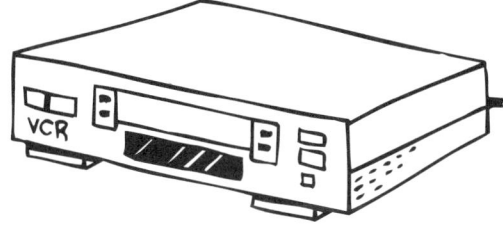

Extra Practice

Directions: Complete each sentence pair with two acronyms from the Word Bank.

1. On Friday, Dad let Aaron stay up until 10:00 _____, since there was no school the next day. On Saturday, Aaron slept until 9:00 _____.

2. My aunt just bought me a new _____ by the singing group Cheetahs Never Prosper. After we listen to it, let's put this African wildlife video in the _____.

3. I wrote _____ and my phone number at the end of my beach party invitation. Then I wrote, _____ *Don't forget to bring a towel!*

4. I wanted to find out about parks in all different parts of the _____. Mom showed me the National Park Service Web site at http://_____.nps.gov.

◎ Vocabulary

Word Play

Directions: Write an acronym from the Word Bank on each blank line. Use the clues to help you. **Hint:** You will need to write one acronym twice.

Word Bank
A.M.
CD
P.M.
P.S.
R.S.V.P.
U.S.A.
VCR
www

1. *Dear* comes near a letter's <u>beginning</u>. _____ comes near a letter's <u>end</u>.

2. A _____ plays <u>movies</u>. A <u>compact disk player</u> plays _____s.

3. You write _____ at the end of an <u>invitation</u>. You write _____ at the end of a <u>letter</u>.

4. A <u>ZIP</u> code is part of a <u>mailing address</u>. _____ is part of a <u>Web address</u>.

5. _____ stands for <u>morning</u>. _____ stands for <u>afternoon and evening</u>.

6. The _____ is a country in <u>North America</u>. <u>France</u> is a country in <u>Europe</u>.

Write a Phone Message

Directions: Use acronyms from the Word Bank to write an imaginary phone message. Use the example to help you.

Dear Mom,

The repair lady called at 11 <u>A.M.</u> She said that our <u>VCR</u> is fixed. Please pick it up ASAP. (They close at 5 <u>P.M.</u>) Do you want to watch my soccer video with me? It shows the <u>U.S.A.</u> playing against Brazil.

Love,
Pablo

<u>P.S.</u> Can you show me that soccer Web site again? I think its address is <u>www.ussoccer.com</u>, but I'm not sure.

⦿ Vocabulary

High Tech

> ## Word Bank
> Internet   keyboard   monitor   mouse   PC
> printer   software   Web address   Web site

Getting to Know New Words

Directions: Read each sentence. Then choose the best word or phrase to replace the underlined word(s). Circle the letter next to your choice.

1. I'm looking for dinosaur facts <u>on the Internet</u>.
   a. in classroom textbooks
   b. in library books
   c. in museums
   d. on the World Wide Web

2. I use the <u>keyboard</u> to type *Tyrannosaurus Rex* in a search box.
   a. rows of letter keys
   b. library computer
   c. rows of piano keys
   d. point and click tool

3. Like a television, a computer <u>monitor</u> has a square piece of glass on its front.
   a. cord
   b. screen
   c. program
   d. game

4. I moved my <u>mouse</u> to the YES box and clicked <u>on it</u>.
   a. small rodent
   b. point and click tool
   c. computer screen
   d. email

5. Sometimes Mom lets me use her <u>PC</u> to play educational computer games.
   a. private clicker
   b. personal calendar
   c. personal computer
   d. private chamber

6. I used the computer <u>printer</u> to print out my cat story.
   a. machine that prints writing and pictures
   b. machine that finds animals' paw prints
   c. screen
   d. mouse

7. This <u>computer software</u> helps students learn math facts.
   a. toy computer
   b. computer textbook
   c. math and computer teacher
   d. program that runs a computer

8. If you need information on the National Park Service, go to www.nps.gov, <u>its Web address</u>.
   a. the place to find it on the Internet
   b. its mailing address
   c. the city where its headquarters is
   d. its insect and spider zoo

9. This <u>Web site</u> on pets tells what different cat noises mean.
   a. library book
   b. school textbook
   c. place on the Internet
   d. poster in a veterinarian's office

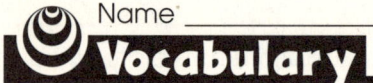
Vocabulary

Vocabulary Practice

Directions: Choose correct words from the Word Bank. Label each part of the diagram and complete the three sentences below it.

Word Bank

Internet
keyboard
monitor
mouse
PC
printer
software
Web address
Web site

MATH SOFTWARE FOR KIDS

1. _____

2. _____

3. _____

4. _____

5. _____

You can use a computer like this one to "surf the Web," or search

the (6)_____. Maybe you can find a

(7)_____ on kangaroos. If you don't have a kangaroo

site's exact (8)_____, type *kangaroo* in a search box.

Extra Practice

Directions: Choose the best way to complete each sentence. Write the correct letter on the line.

1. **PC** stands for personal _____.   a. typing

2. You use a **keyboard** for _____.   b. Web

3. You use a **mouse** for pointing and _____.   c. clicking

4. A **Web site's Web address** usually includes _____.   d. computer

5. A computer **monitor** is like a TV _____.   e. pictures

6. Another name for the **Internet** is the World Wide _____.   f. screen

7. A computer **printer** can print out words and _____.   g. learn

8. Educational computer **software** helps students _____.   h. www

 **Vocabulary**

Word Play

Directions: Use the clues
to solve each riddle with
a word from the Word Bank.

Word Bank		
Internet	mouse	software
keyboard	PC	Web address
monitor	printer	Web site

1. Which word begins like **princess** and ends like **painter**?

   _____

2. I begin like **keyword** and end like **skateboard**. Which word am I?

   _____

3. Name an acronym that begins like **P.S.** and ends like **Washington, D.C.**

   _____

4. Which word begins like **interest** and ends like **hornet**?

   _____

5. I squeak, point, and click. I rhyme with **house**. Which word am I?

   _____

6. I begin like a spider's food catcher. I contain the words **add** and **dress**. Write me on this line:

   _____

7. I begin like **webfoot** and end like **campsite**. Which word am I?

   _____

8. Which word begins like **softer** and ends like **cookware**?

   _____

9. I almost (but don't really) rhyme with **thermometer**. Which word am I?

   _____

Write a Radio Advertisement

Directions: Use a few words from the Word Bank to write an ad you might
hear on the radio. Use the example for help.

Man's voice: Oh, *NO!* My <u>PC</u> just crashed! I've lost a whole day's work!

Woman's voice: What do you see on your <u>monitor</u>?

Man: A black screen with red letters that say, "SORRY, YOUR COMPUTER JUST
DIED. MAY IT REST IN PEACE."

Woman: Sounds like it's time to call the Computer Doc.

Man: The Computer Doc?

Woman: That's right! Remember last week, when I couldn't log onto the <u>Internet</u>?
Well, the Computer Doc fixed the problem as quick as a <u>mouse</u> click.

Man: Maybe the Computer Doc can fix *my* PC, too. Does he make house calls?

Woman: Of course he does! Just call 1-800-CDOCTOR.

Vocabulary

Can You Hear Me?

Word Bank

bellowed	boasted	exclaimed
mumble	murmur	remarks
summoned	urged	

Getting to Know New Words

Directions: Read each sentence. Then choose the best word or phrase to replace the underlined word(s). Circle the letter next to your choice.

1. "Line up RIGHT AWAY!" <u>bellowed</u> the army officer.
   - a. whispered
   - b. suggested
   - c. yelled
   - d. said

2. Brittany <u>boasted</u> that her family was the richest one in town.
   - a. bragged
   - b. wondered whether
   - c. thought
   - d. felt shy about saying

3. "Great news!" Mom <u>exclaimed</u>.
   - a. said quietly
   - b. shrieked angrily
   - c. said excitedly
   - d. said tiredly

4. If you want me to understand what you're saying, don't <u>mumble</u>.
   - a. speak so loudly
   - b. argue with me
   - c. speak softly in a way that is hard to hear
   - d. whisper loudly in an angry, hissing voice

5. From down the hallway we heard the <u>murmur</u> of conversation.
   - a. soft growl
   - b. loud laughter
   - c. sudden, excited shouting
   - d. muffled, ongoing sound

6. Please keep your <u>remarks</u> to yourself—no one asked for your opinion.
   - a. comments
   - b. stories
   - c. slang words
   - d. laughter

7. King Durwood <u>summoned</u> his servant and demanded breakfast.
   - a. called
   - b. scolded
   - c. sent away
   - d. talked with

8. I <u>urged</u> Jill not to ride her bike without wearing a helmet.
   - a. ordered
   - b. said to
   - c. tried to persuade
   - d. sent Jill an email that said

Vocabulary

Vocabulary Practice

Directions: Choose the best word from the Word Bank to complete each sentence or group.

1. The company president _____ her workers to an important meeting.

2. If you make rude _____ in class, you will have to stay in at recess time.

3. Through the forest we heard the _____ of a rushing river.

4. Some people _____ their words when they feel shy or confused.

5. suggested, persuaded, convinced, _____

6. yelled, shouted, howled, _____

7. "I'm going to win the talent show!" Taylor _____.

8. "Wow, what a surprise!" Marcy _____.

Word Bank			
bellowed	boasted	exclaimed	mumble
murmur	remarks	summoned	urged

Extra Practice

Directions: Choose the best way to complete each sentence. Write the correct letter on the line.

1. The school principal **summoned** the teachers to _____.   a. careful

2. Mom and Dad **urged** me to be _____.   b. a bull

3. Through the wall I could hear the **murmur** of _____.   c. opinion

4. When people **mumble**, they don't speak _____.   d. conceited

5. "Hey, listen to this!" Emma **exclaimed** _____.   e. a meeting

6. When a bee stung me, I **bellowed** like _____.   f. suddenly

7. Joe **boasted** so much that everyone said he was _____.   g. the TV

8. Don't make any **remarks** unless someone asks for your _____.   h. clearly

Word Play

Directions: Use the clues to solve each riddle with a word from the Word Bank.

Word Bank		
bellowed	exclaimed	murmur
boasted	mumble	remarks
summoned		urged

1. Which word begins like **exclude** and ends with **aimed**?

_____

2. Name a synonym for **mutter** that rhymes with **tumble**.

_____

3. Name an antonym for **whispered** that rhymes with **yellowed**.

_____

4. Which word begins like **urgent** and rhymes with **merged**?

_____

5. Which word begins like **summary** and ends like **buttoned**?

_____

6. Name a synonym for **bragged** that rhymes with **toasted**.

_____

7. I'm six letters long, but I contain only *m, r,* and *u.* Which word am I?

_____

8. Which word begins like **remain** and end like **sparks**?

_____

Write a Folktale

Directions: Use at least three words from the Word Bank to write the first few paragraphs of a folktale with animal characters. Use the example to help you. If you have time, finish your folktale.

The Buffalo and the Prairie Dog

A buffalo was galloping across the plains when he stepped in a prairie dog hole and tripped. "OUCH!" he bellowed as he crashed to the earth with a great thud. Six feet underground a mother prairie dog was feeding her pups. The buffalo's fall shook the family's burrow, causing part of the ceiling to fall.

"My goodness!" the mother exclaimed. But before she went upstairs to see what had happened, she urged her children not to utter a sound. Who knew what danger lurked outside?

 **Vocabulary**

Tusks, Talons, and Tentacles

Word Bank			
antlers	burrow	galloped	jaguar
scurry	talons	tentacles	tusks

Getting to Know New Words

Directions: Read each sentence. Then choose the best word or phrase to replace the underlined word(s). Circle the letter next to your choice.

1. A male deer grows a new pair of underlined antlers each year.
   a. bright eyes
   b. furry ears
   c. branching horns
   d. front hooves

2. The rabbit family lives in an underground burrow.
   a. hole
   b. hive
   c. stream
   d. nest

3. The frightened horses galloped across the prairie.
   a. walked
   b. strolled
   c. ran
   d. trotted

4. Closely related to the lion, the American jaguar is a fierce meat eater.
   a. big cat
   b. bison
   c. eagle
   d. squirrel

5. I saw a scared mouse scurry into its hole.
   a. move carelessly
   b. move hurriedly
   c. somersault
   d. zigzag

6. A grizzly bear has deadly talons on all four of its paws.
   a. claws
   b. poison
   c. fangs
   d. quills

7. An octopus has eight squiggly tentacles.
   a. eyes
   b. ears
   c. long, thin body parts
   d. short, thick body parts

8. An elephant has two long, pointed tusks.
   a. claws
   b. quills
   c. large teeth that stick out of its mouth
   d. big, floppy ears that it uses to fan itself

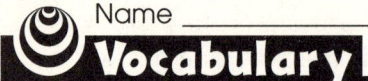

Vocabulary

creature-related nouns and verbs

Vocabulary Practice

Directions: Write the word from the Word Bank that best completes each group.

1. lion, tiger, cheetah, _____

2. claws, eagle's, tiger's, _____

3. home, tunnel, underground, _____

4. pointed, ivory, elephant's, _____

5. horse, ran, raced, _____

6. scuttle, scamper, hurry, _____

7. long, squiggly, octopus's, _____

8. horns, deer's, moose's, _____

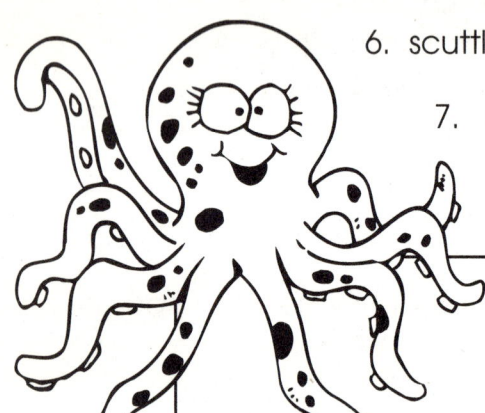

Word Bank

antlers	burrow	galloped	jaguar
scurry	talons	tentacles	tusks

Extra Practice

Directions: Choose the best way to answer the question or complete the sentence. Write the correct letter on the line.

1. An octopus uses its **tentacles** to grab its _____. a. teeth

2. Like other big cats, the **jaguar** is a _____. b. scared

3. An elephant's **tusks** are oversized _____. c. prey

4. An owl uses its sharp **talons** for _____. d. reindeer

5. Squirrels **scurry** away when they are _____. e. digging

6. A rabbit creates its **burrow** by _____. f. carnivore

7. Animals with **antlers** include moose and _____. g. quickly

8. The zebra **galloped** away, moving _____. h. hunting

⊙ Vocabulary

Word Play

Directions: Write a word from the Word Bank on each blank line. Use the clues to help you. **Hint:** Write one word twice.

Word Bank

antlers	galloped	scurry
burrow	jaguar	talons
tentacles		tusks

1. A <u>fox</u> lives in a <u>den</u>. A <u>rabbit</u> lives in a _____.

2. When the <u>horse</u> sped up, it _____.
   When <u>mice</u> speed up, they _____.

3. An <u>eagle</u> has sharp _____ on its feet.
   A <u>cow</u> has a <u>hoof</u> on each foot.

4. A <u>goat</u> has <u>horns</u> on its head.
   A <u>deer</u> has _____ on its head.

5. An <u>octopus</u> uses its _____ for hunting.
   A <u>tiger</u> uses its _____ for hunting.

6. A <u>grizzly</u> is a kind of <u>bear</u>.
   A _____ is a kind of <u>big cat</u>.

7. <u>Elephants</u> have special body parts called _____.
   <u>Kangaroos</u> have special body parts called <u>pouches</u>.

Write a Magazine Advertisement

Directions: Using a few words from the Word Bank, write an ad that will attract visitors to a wildlife park. Use the example to help you.

For wild creatures galore...
slither, pounce, gallop, or <u>scurry</u> down Highway 19
to Ralph's Rhino Rancho.

Have you ever watched a <u>jaguar</u> sharpening her <u>talons</u> on a tree?
Has a herd of zebra ever <u>galloped</u> across your path?
Have you ever met a moose with huge <u>antlers</u>?
Experience all this and more at Ralph's Rancho.
And don't miss our star attraction:
twin baby RHINOS named RYAN and RHIANNON!!
Only $20 admission per vehicle.

29

Let's Get Wet!

Word Bank			
blotted	evaporate	goggles	moisten
seep	squirt	surf	vessel

Getting to Know New Words

Directions: Read each sentence. Then choose the best word or phrase to replace the underlined word(s). Circle the letter next to your choice.

1. As she wept, Sierra <u>blotted</u> her tears with a tissue.
   a. soaked up
   b. shut off
   c. plugged up
   d. smeared

2. If you boil water, it will <u>evaporate</u>.
   a. freeze
   b. melt
   c. turn into steam
   d. turn into soup

3. When I swim, I wear <u>goggles</u> over my eyes.
   a. sunglasses
   b. binoculars with a strap
   c. a baseball cap
   d. protective glasses

4. You can <u>moisten</u> a stamp with your tongue or a wet sponge.
   a. wet
   b. dry
   c. stick on
   d. ruin

5. Over time, rainwater will <u>seep</u> down into the ground.
   a. burrow
   b. flow quickly
   c. flow slowly
   d. dig

6. Dad likes to <u>squirt us</u> with the garden hose on hot summer days.
   a. clean us
   b. tease us
   c. spray water on us
   d. help us water plants

7. We walked on the beach and listened to the soft roar of the <u>surf</u>.
   a. waves breaking
   b. whales calling
   c. sea lions roaring
   d. blowing sand

8. The <u>vessel</u> carried passengers and supplies across the ocean.
   a. ship
   b. train
   c. carriage
   d. bus

Vocabulary Practice

Directions: Write the word from the Word Bank that best completes each group or sentence.

1. ship, boat, ocean, _____

2. beach, waves, crash, _____

3. steam, vapor, rise, _____

4. glasses, protective, swimming, _____

5. If we don't repair the wall, rainwater could _____ through the cracks.

6. After exercising, Michael _____ his sweaty face with a towel.

7. To seal an envelope, you must _____ the glue on the flap.

8. My little brothers like to take mouthfuls of water and _____ it at each other.

Word Bank			
blotted	evaporate	goggles	moisten
seep	squirt	surf	vessel

Extra Practice

Directions: Choose the best way to answer the question or complete the sentence. Write the correct letter on the line.

1. What is one type of **vessel**? _____   a. towel

2. When water **evaporates**, it _____.   b. oil or eggs

3. People wear **goggles** to protect their _____.   c. a cargo ship

4. What can you use to **moisten** cookie dough? _____   d. the soil

5. What can you use to **squirt** water? _____   e. the beach

6. You see and hear the **surf** at _____.   f. rises

7. When you water a garden, water **seeps** into _____.   g. eyes

8. I **blotted** my wet skin with a _____.   h. a hose

◎ Vocabulary

Word Play

Directions: Write a word from the Word Bank to fit each clue. Find out what the Spanish phrase *las tormentas* means.

Word Bank	
blotted	squirt
evaporate	surf
goggles	vessel
moisten	broth
seep	swamp

1. Soup
2. Vaporize
3. Spurt
4. Wet

5. Ship
6. Soaked up
7. Eyewear
8. _____board

9. Wetland
10. Ooze

1. ___ ___ ___ ___ ___ ___
2. ___ ___ ___ ___ ___ ___ ___ ___
3. ___ ___ ___ ___ ___
4. ___ ___ ___
5. ___ ___ ___ ___
6. ___ ___ ___ ___ ___ ___
7. ___ ___ ___ ___ ___ ___ ___
8. ___ ___ ___ ___
9. ___ ___ ___ ___ ___
10. ___ ___ ___ ___

Write a TV Weather Report

Directions: Use a few words from the Word Bank to write a weather report that you might hear on the TV news. Use the example to help you.

News Anchorwoman: And now it's time to hear from Wally the Wacky Weatherman. What's the forecast, Wally? Will I need to carry an umbrella on my way to the bus stop tomorrow?

Wally: Yep, it sure looks that way, Delia. We've got an ugly storm brewing off our coastline. And it's not just going to moisten our community with a few drops—it'll be a real downpour. For all you sailors listening, especially those with smaller vessels, here's my advice: stay on shore! There'll be heavy surf and high winds. Bad news for sports fans, too: the city ballpark will be a swamp this weekend. The good news is that the puddles *will* evaporate—after a month or so. That's about it, Delia. Stay dry tomorrow!

Anchorwoman: I'll sure try, Wally! And now, here's Courtney Porter with sports.

Vocabulary

Homophones

Aa Bb C~~~ Fe

Word Bank			
allowed	aloud	ceiling	foul
fowl	idle	idol	sealing

About homophones: Homophones are words like *allowed* and *aloud*. They sound the same but have different spellings and meanings.

Getting to Know New Words

Directions: Read each sentence. Then choose the best word or phrase to replace the underlined word(s). Circle the letter next to your choice.

1. Most four-year-olds aren't <u>allowed</u> to cross the street by themselves.
   a. able
   b. smart enough
   c. given permission
   d. careless enough

2. After lunch, our teacher reads <u>aloud</u> to us from a chapter book.
   a. very loudly
   b. silently
   c. out loud
   d. in Spanish

3. Dad painted the kitchen walls blue and the <u>ceiling</u> white.
   a. floor
   b. cupboards
   c. frame around the doorway
   d. room's top inside surface

4. When I cracked open the rotten egg, a <u>foul</u> odor filled the kitchen.
   a. fragrant
   b. horrid
   c. spicy
   d. faint

5. Our neighbor has a new pet that clucks or quacks—it must be some kind of <u>fowl</u>.
   a. chicken, duck, or turkey
   b. parakeet, parrot, or canary
   c. snake or lizard
   d. frog or toad

6. <u>Idle</u> people who watch TV for hours are sometimes called couch potatoes.
   a. silly
   b. sleepy
   c. lazy
   d. plump

7. I respect my mom more than anyone else—she is my <u>idol</u>.
   a. mother
   b. hero
   c. friend
   d. like a sister to me

8. <u>Sealing</u> an envelope is easy—you just lick the flap and smooth it down.
   a. closing
   b. stuffing
   c. opening
   d. flapping

33

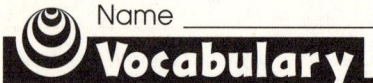
Vocabulary Practice

Directions: Write the word from the Word Bank that best completes each group.

Word Bank
allowed
aloud
ceiling
foul
fowl
idle
idol
sealing

1. horrible, awful, terrible, _____
2. permitted, legal, okay, _____
3. floor, wall, roof, _____
4. chicken, turkey, duck, _____
5. **Busy** and **active** are antonyms for _____.
6. **Silently** is an antonym for _____.
7. hero, celebrity, leader, _____
8. gluing, taping, closing, _____

Extra Practice

Directions: Complete each sentence pair with two homophones from the Word Bank.

1. My hardworking dad is almost never _____, but he knows how to have fun too. When I grow up I want to be just like him—he's my _____.

2. We're _____ up all the little cracks in the walls before we paint them. We need to borrow a ladder so we can reach the _____ too.

3. The weather has been really _____ lately—it won't stop raining. Even Grandma's _____s are inside the chicken coop trying to stay dry.

4. I used to read _____ most of the time, but now I usually read silently to myself. On each library visit, we're _____ to check out ten books each.

Word Play

Directions: Write a word from the Word Bank on each blank line. Use the clues to help you. Capitalize words that begin sentences.

Word Bank		
allowed	aloud	ceiling
foul	fowl	idle
idol	sealing	

1. A <u>floor</u> is the <u>bottom</u> part of a room. A _____ is the <u>top</u> part of a room.

2. <u>Roses</u> smell <u>fragrant</u>. <u>Garbage</u> smells _____.

3. <u>Rewarded</u> is an antonym for <u>punished</u>. _____ is an antonym for <u>forbidden</u>.

4. You use <u>paper</u> for <u>wrapping</u> a package. You use <u>tape</u> for _____ a package.

5. A <u>jaguar</u> is a kind of <u>big cat</u>. A <u>turkey</u> is a kind of _____.

6. When you're <u>silent</u>, you don't <u>talk</u>. When you're _____, you don't <u>work</u>.

7. <u>Villain</u> and <u>creep</u> are synonyms. <u>Hero</u> and _____ are synonyms too.

8. When you read <u>silently</u>, you read to <u>yourself</u>. When you read _____, you read to <u>others</u>.

Write a Joke

Directions: Use two homophones from the Word Bank to write a joke that plays with word meanings. Use the example to help you.

Silence in the Library!

Question: Pablo saw a gigantic sign in the library. What did it say?

Answer:

Talking Is NOT ALOUD!

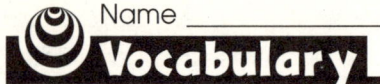
Review

Directions: Read the story. Then choose the best answer to each question about an underlined word. Circle the letter next to your answer.

Volunteering at the Vet's

My Aunt Ursula is a <u>veterinarian</u>, and last summer she said I could work as a <u>volunteer</u> in her busy office. "You're young," Aunt Ursi remarked, "but you're <u>mature</u> for your age." (I'm thirteen, a pupil at Lyndon B. Johnson Middle School.) I got to wear a white cotton lab coat just like a real vet's and an identification <u>badge</u> that said: *Hi, I'm David, an Albany Vet Clinic Volunteer.*

I worked three mornings a week. The clinic opened at 8 <u>A.M.</u>, but I had to be there at 7 to clean up the waiting rooms. There were two—one said *Cats* on the door and the other said *Dogs*. Aunt Ursi told me to sweep and mop the *Dogs* room first so the dampness would <u>evaporate</u> by the time patients started to arrive. I thought this was to avoid accidents due to <u>slick</u> floors, but it turned out to be dogs' muddy footprints that concerned my aunt.

Cats' footprints are not much of a problem, since cats usually hide in their carrying cases or burrow beneath their owners' jackets. Most cats hate going to the vet. To them, an <u>annual</u> checkup is an outrageous insult rather than an everyday event.

One of my jobs was to lead dogs or carry cats from one examining room to another. This doesn't sound difficult, I know, but put yourself in my place. Picture this: You're carrying a struggling cat named Puffball, who suddenly digs her needle-sharp talons into your neck. Bellowing with pain, you drop the spitting, growling bundle of fur to the floor. Puffball scurries down the hallway and takes a flying leap onto a countertop. From there she hops to the top of a tall filing cabinet. Holding up a handful of Yummee Treetz 4 Katz, you urge her to "Please come down, nice kitty! Here, kitty, kitty! *Pleeeease* come down!" From her perch up near the ceiling, Puffball hisses disgustedly. You blot your sweaty forehead on the sleeve of your white lab coat.

On the Monday of my third week at the clinic, Aunt Ursi summoned me into her office. She was sitting behind her PC monitor gazing at an angry email from Puffball's mommy and daddy. "I hear you had a little problem with a cat," she said.

"Yes, ma'am," I mumbled. The remainder of my time at Albany Vet Clinic was spent sealing envelopes and pasting stamps on "Time for a checkup!" letters. And I was still allowed to mop floors, of course.

1. Veterinarians are animal _____.
   a. trainers
   b. lovers and pet owners
   c. doctors
   d. control officers

2. Since David is a volunteer, he probably isn't _____.
   a. paid for his work
   b. very helpful to his aunt
   c. very smart
   d. a pet owner

3. When Aunt Ursi calls David "mature for your age" she means that he is _____.
   a. a grown man
   b. a responsible boy
   c. a year older than she is
   d. a crazy teenager

4. David probably wears his identification badge _____.
   a. pinned to his coat
   b. on his head
   c. tied around his waist
   d. on his wrist

5. The clinic opens at 8 A.M., or _____.
   a. about eight minutes late
   b. eight o'clock in the morning
   c. eight o'clock in the evening
   d. eight hours per day

6. Why does Aunt Ursi want the dampness to evaporate from the floor before the dogs and their owners arrive?
   a. so the water and the dogs' dirty feet won't create mud
   b. so the dryness and the dogs' dirty feet won't create dust
   c. so the dogs won't slip on the dry, slick floor
   d. so the owners won't slip on the wet, slick floor

7. What might cause a slick floor?
   a. mopping it
   b. drying it
   c. covering it with a rug
   d. cats' footprints

8. A pet's annual checkup happens _____.
   a. once a week
   b. once a month
   c. once a year
   d. after five years

9. Puffball's talons are her _____.
   a. teeth
   b. claws
   c. birdlike feet
   d. footprints

10. Which is a synonym for bellowing, as it is used in this story?
    a. snorting
    b. growling
    c. yelling
    d. murmuring

Vocabulary

11. When Puffball <u>scurries</u> down the hallway, she is moving _____.
   a. wearily
   b. angrily
   c. carefully
   d. quickly

12. David <u>urges</u> Puffball to come down. In other words, he _____.
   a. tries to persuade her to come down
   b. hopes to trick her into coming down
   c. invites her to come down
   d. commands her to come down

13. Puffball is near the <u>ceiling</u> because _____.
   a. she flew up there
   b. David put her in the highest cage
   c. she is on top of a tall cabinet
   d. she is a fierce, angry cat

14. Puffball <u>hisses</u> to show that she _____.
   a. forgives David
   b. wants a treat
   c. is angry or scared
   d. likes being way up high

15. David <u>blots</u> his forehead to _____.
   a. soak up the sweat
   b. dry up the water
   c. wash it off
   d. show that he is puzzled

16. David's coat <u>sleeves</u> cover his _____.
   a. face
   b. ears
   c. arms
   d. legs

17. Aunt Ursi's <u>PC</u> is her _____.
   a. patient
   b. computer
   c. veterinary clinic
   d. white lab coat

18. A <u>monitor</u> is a computer _____.
   a. screen
   b. mouse
   c. keyboard
   d. printer

19. Why does David <u>mumble</u> when he says "Yes, ma'am"?
   a. He is angry with Aunt Ursi, so he speaks loudly and rudely.
   b. He is embarrassed, so it is hard to understand his speech.
   c. He isn't used to calling his aunt "ma'am," and he sounds stiff.
   d. His voice is very deep and tired, so it sounds like thunder.

20. What is another way to say <u>sealing</u>, as it is used in this story?
   a. folding
   b. organizing
   c. wetting the flaps and smoothing them down
   d. licking the stamps and sticking them down

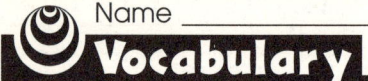 Vocabulary

Don't Be So Unfriendly!

Word Bank			
banish	coax	condemned	contempt
dispute	hostile	quarreled	suspicion

Getting to Know New Words

Directions: Read each sentence. Then choose the best word or phrase to replace the underlined word(s). Circle the letter next to your choice.

1. The king had the power to <u>banish criminals from</u> his kingdom.
   a. stop criminals from entering
   b. make criminals leave
   c. find and punish any criminals in
   d. stop criminals from doing business in

2. I tried to <u>coax</u> my cat to come down from a tall tree.
   a. convince
   b. force
   c. order
   d. pay

3. In her speech, the principal <u>condemned</u> bullies who harm younger students.
   a. excused
   b. criticized
   c. named
   d. ignored

4. Charlotte has great <u>contempt</u> for people who mistreat animals.
   a. sympathy
   b. pity
   c. plans
   d. scorn

5. My friends are having an angry <u>dispute</u>, but I am trying to keep out of it.
   a. conversation
   b. argument
   c. email exchange
   d. chat

6. Ever since our disagreement, Taylor has acted <u>hostile</u> toward me.
   a. strangely
   b. respectfully
   c. friendly
   d. unfriendly

7. My sister and I <u>quarreled</u> a lot when we were little, but now we get along pretty well.
   a. played
   b. cried
   c. argued
   d. misbehaved

8. The thief did nothing to cause <u>suspicion</u>, so no one realized that she had stolen the jewels.
   a. people to distrust her
   b. people to trust her
   c. people to dislike her
   d. an argument

 Vocabulary

Vocabulary Practice

Directions: Write the word from the Word Bank that best completes each group or sentence.

1. I have a _____ that Jack is the one who hid my sweater.

2. People _____ the movie, calling it the worst film they had ever seen.

3. scorn, disrespect, disgust, _____

4. angry, unfriendly, cold, _____

5. argued, bickered, squabbled, _____

6. fight, conflict, argument, _____

7. **Welcome** is an antonym for _____.

8. plead, convince, persuade, _____

Word Bank			
banish	coax	condemned	contempt
dispute	hostile	quarreled	suspicion

Extra Practice

Directions: Choose the best way to complete each sentence or answer each question. Write the correct letter on the line.

1. A **hostile** act is not _____.

2. The friends **quarreled**, and then they _____.

3. If someone arouses your **suspicion**, you don't _____.

4. What does "I **banish** you from my kingdom!" mean? _____

5. How do you feel when you're in a **dispute** with someone? _____

6. What might you say to **coax** someone to do something? _____

7. The judge **condemned** a man to prison after he was found _____.

8. When you feel **contempt** for someone's opinion, you think it is _____.

a. guilty

b. foolish

c. trust him

d. made up

e. friendly

f. "Please!"

g. angry

h. "Get out!'

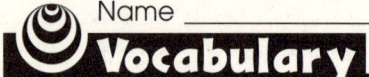 Vocabulary

Word Play

Directions: Write a word from the Word Bank to fit each clue. Find out what can help you tell right from wrong.

Word Bank			
accuse	banish	contempt	quarreled
admit	coax	dispute	suspicion
	condemned	hostile	

1. Point the finger at   ___ ___ ___ ___ ___ ___

2. Unfriendly   ___ ___ ___ ___ ___ ___ ___

3. Send away   ___ ___ ___ ___ ___ ___

4. Argument   ___ ___ ___ ___ ___ ___ ___

5. Persuade   ___ ___ ___ ___

6. Confess   ___ ___ ___ ___ ___

7. Criticized   ___ ___ ___ ___ ___ ___ ___ ___ ___

8. Scorn   ___ ___ ___ ___ ___ ___ ___ ___

9. Mistrust   ___ ___ ___ ___ ___ ___ ___ ___ ___

10. Squabbled   ___ ___ ___ ___ ___ ___ ___ ___

Write an Argument

Directions: Use a few words from the Word Bank to write a conversation between two neighbors who are involved in a dispute. Use the example to help you.

A Phone Conversation

Ms. Grump: Hello, Mr. Magillacutty?

Mr. Magillacutty: Ms. Grump, it's midnight! I don't mean to accuse you of rudeness, but can't this wait until morning?

Ms. G: (in a hostile tone) No, it can't! I've never quarreled with a neighbor before, but that noisy dog of yours is keeping me awake.

Mr. M: Well, I've never been involved in a dispute with a neighbor, either! I admit that Babette barks occasionally, but—

Ms. G: (in a voice filled with contempt) Occasionally! Ha!

Mr. M: (beginning to get upset) Well, what do you plan to do about it? Banish me and my poor puppy from the neighborhood?

Ms. G: (a little embarrassed, trying to coax him to calm down) Of course I didn't mean that—I just want a little peace and quiet!

Vocabulary   science-related nouns, verbs, and adjectives

The World Around Us

Word Bank			
blizzard	copper	crater	decayed
equator	evergreen	fossil	wilt

Getting to Know New Words

Directions: Read each sentence. Then choose the best word or phrase to replace the underlined word(s). Circle the letter next to your choice.

1. *The Long Winter* tells of a pioneer family enduring <u>blizzard</u> after <u>blizzard</u> in a small northern town.
   a. snowstorm
   b. earthquake
   c. hardship
   d. attack

2. Pennies used to be made of solid <u>copper</u>, but today they have zinc inside.
   a. silver metal
   b. shiny stainless steel
   c. reddish-brown metal
   d. white gold metal

3. Long ago, a meteor hit the earth and formed this <u>crater</u>.
   a. mountaintop
   b. river valley
   c. Grand Canyon
   d. bowl-shaped area

4. Over time, the dead leaves <u>decayed</u> and turned into soil.
   a. blew away
   b. dissolved
   c. rotted
   d. shattered

5. Near the earth's <u>equator</u>, the climate is very hot and wet.
   a. icecaps
   b. north pole
   c. south pole
   d. middle

6. All pines are <u>evergreen trees</u>.
   a. neon green trees
   b. young trees
   c. trees that stay green all year
   d. trees whose leaves fall in the autumn

7. This snail shell imprint is an ancient <u>fossil</u>.
   a. trace of a living thing found in rock
   b. artwork that cave dwellers painted on rock walls
   c. symbol
   d. tool

8. Even in water, cut flowers <u>wilt</u> after a few days.
   a. stink
   b. droop
   c. dry up
   d. turn into soil

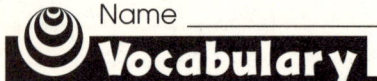 **Vocabulary**

science-related nouns, verbs, and adjectives

Vocabulary Practice

Directions: Write the word from the Word Bank that best completes each group or sentence.

1. rotted, spoiled, decomposed, _____

2. Over millions of years the dinosaur bone became a

   _____.

3. get limp, droop, sag, _____

4. Pines, spruces, holly trees, and others are _____ trees.

5. The volcano's top exploded, forming a _____.

6. gold, silver, zinc, _____

7. hurricane, tornado, hailstorm, _____

8. An imaginary circle around the earth's middle is called the

   _____.

Word Bank			
blizzard	copper	crater	decayed
equator	evergreen	fossil	wilt

Extra Practice

Directions: Choose the best way to complete each sentence. Write the correct letter on the line.

1. When celery **wilts**, it gets limp and _____.   a. snow

2. The **equator** is midway between the north and south _____.   b. holly

3. As the oranges **decayed**, they became _____.   c. moldy

4. I found an insect **fossil** in a piece of _____.   d. bowl

5. A moon **crater** is shaped like a huge _____.   e. poles

6. We use **copper** to make pennies and _____.   f. pots

7. **Evergreen** plants without needles include _____.   g. droopy

8. After the **blizzard**, the town was blanketed with _____.   h. rock

Word Play

Directions: Use the clues to solve each riddle with a word from the Word Bank.

Word Bank		
blizzard	crater	equator
copper	decayed	evergreen
fossil		wilt

1. Which word begins like **decal** and ends like **played**?

    _____

2. I'm a storm that rhymes with **lizard**. Which word am I?

    _____

3. Name a synonym for **droop** that rhymes with **quilt**.

    _____

4. I begin like **foster**. I rhyme the last two syllables of **colossal**. Which word am I?

    _____

5. I'm shaped like a bowl, and I rhyme with **greater**. Which word am I?

    _____

6. I'm penny-colored, and I rhyme with **whopper**. Which word am I?

    _____

7. My first part rhymes with **clever**, and my second rhymes with **queen**. Which word am I?

    _____

8. Which word begins like **equal** and ends like **alligator**?

    _____

Write an Acrostic Poem

Directions: Use a word from the Word Bank to write an acrostic poem. Use the example for help.

Blizzard

B lowing winds

L oudly HOWLING!

I nside we're warm and cozy.

Z ero degrees Fahrenheit or colder.

Z ero chance of school tomorrow.

A fter it's over, we'll see a world of white.

R ivers, streams, and ponds frozen solid.

D ark at four in the afternoon.

Good Night, Sleep Tight!

Word Bank			
arouse	drowsy	exhausted	lullaby
moonbeam	nestle	nightingale	retire

Getting to Know New Words

Directions: Read each sentence. Then choose the best word or phrase to replace the underlined word(s). Circle the letter next to your choice.

1. Barking dogs and clanging trashcans <u>arouse</u> even deep sleepers.
   a. annoy
   b. anger
   c. wake up
   d. calm

2. Reading at bedtime makes me <u>drowsy</u> enough to fall asleep.
   a. smart
   b. warm
   c. happy
   d. sleepy

3. When I spent the night at my friend's house I got little sleep, so I came home <u>exhausted</u>.
   a. excited
   b. very tired
   c. grumpy
   d. refreshed

4. Each night Mom sings a <u>lullaby</u> to my baby brother.
   a. nursery rhyme
   b. rhyming song
   c. comforting song
   d. silly song

5. A pale <u>moonbeam</u> streamed through the window, lighting the dark room.
   a. light from a street lamp
   b. ray of moonlight
   c. ray of starlight
   d. glow from a nightlight

6. Newborn kittens <u>nestle</u> against their mother when they sleep.
   a. lie close
   b. snore softly
   c. push gently
   d. purr loudly

7. At ten P.M., a <u>nightingale</u> began singing outside Emma's bedroom window.
   a. cat
   b. friend
   c. relative
   d. bird

8. This evening I'm so tired that I plan to <u>retire</u> early.
   a. go to bed
   b. finish my work
   c. wake up
   d. eat dinner

Vocabulary

Vocabulary Practice

Directions: Write the word from the Word Bank that best completes each group.

1. moonlight, starlight, sunbeam,

   _____

2. burrow, snuggle, cuddle,

   _____

3. weak, dog-tired, drained, _____

4. soothing, bedtime, cradlesong, _____

5. thrush, mockingbird, canary, _____

6. dozy, sleepy, nodding, _____

7. startle, excite, wake up, _____

8. hit the sack, go beddie-bye, _____

Word Bank
arouse
drowsy
exhausted
lullaby
moonbeam
nestle
nightingale
retire

Extra Practice

Directions: Choose the best way to complete each sentence or answer each question. Write the correct letter on the line.

1. When do fourth graders **retire** on school nights? _____

2. What can a **nightingale** do, besides sing? _____

3. One famous **lullaby** is called "Rock-a-bye _____."

4. Compared with a sunbeam, a **moonbeam** is _____.

5. What might **arouse** a sleeping baby? _____

6. Puppies **nestle** close to their _____.

7. What can make people feel **drowsy**? _____

8. What expression means **exhausted**? _____

a. Baby

b. littermates

c. fly

d. 8 or 9 o'clock

e. loud music

f. tuckered out

g. cool

h. boredom

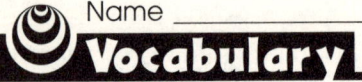

Word Play

Directions: Use the clues to complete the crossword puzzle with words from the Word Bank.

DOWN

1. Lunar ray
3. Songbird
4. Cradlesong
6. Awaken
7. Flicker

ACROSS

2. Catnap
5. Dog-tired
8. Sleepy
9. Call it a day
10. Cuddle

Word Bank

arouse	nestle
drowsy	nightingale
exhausted	retire
lullaby	snooze
moonbeam	twinkle

Write a Lullaby

Directions: Choose words from the Word Bank to write lyrics for a lullaby. You can write a silly song if you like. Use the example to help you.

The Nightingale's Song

Twinkle stars and moonbeams shine,

Take a snooze, oh baby mine!

Please don't weep, and don't you wail,

Just listen to the song of the nightingale.

Drowsy babe, exhausted mom

Driftin' away to the night bird's song.

Vocabulary

How Do You Feel About Synonyms?

Word Bank

ashamed	astonished	dejected
	enthusiastic	glum
	guilty	thrilled

Getting to Know New Words

Directions: Read each sentence. Then choose the best word or phrase to replace the underlined word(s). Circle the letter next to your choice.

1. I'm <u>ashamed of</u> my impolite behavior at Grandma's house.
   a. amused by
   b. upset about
   c. not terribly sorry for
   d. embarrassed about

2. I had no idea that Shelby was such a good gymnast, so her performance <u>astonished me</u>.
   a. surprised me very much
   b. was very disappointing
   c. filled me with joy
   d. made me jealous

3. When we leave home without her, our dog looks so <u>dejected</u>.
   a. happy
   b. sad
   c. confused
   d. bored

4. The art students were <u>enthusiastic</u> about their wonderful new project.
   a. excited
   b. wondering
   c. asking
   d. confused

5. Please don't look so <u>glum</u>—you can visit your friend another time.
   a. unhappy
   b. relieved
   c. bored
   d. surprised

6. I felt <u>guilty</u> about breaking my brother's toy, but I didn't confess that I'd done it.
   a. depressed
   b. sorry
   c. scared
   d. glad

7. I'm <u>thrilled</u> about seeing my grandparents again after all this time.
   a. nervous
   b. sorry
   c. excited
   d. wondering

Vocabulary

Vocabulary Practice

Directions: Find the synonym pairs. For each word from the Word Bank, write another one with a similar meaning.

1. thrilled _____   2. guilty _____   3. glum _____

Directions: Use the words you paired in items 1–3. Complete each two sentences by writing a synonym pair.

4. I scolded our dog, "You should be

   _____

   of yourself for eating garbage out of the trashcan." The poor thing did look

   _____,

   so I forgave her.

5. From your

   _____

   expression, I can tell that you have heard the sad news. But don't feel so

   _____

   —maybe our team will win next time.

6. An

   _____,

   cheering crowd greeted the popular singing star. We were all so

   _____

   to see her in person!

```
                    Word Bank
 ashamed      astonished      dejected
      enthusiastic        glum
         guilty        thrilled
```

Extra Practice

Directions: Complete the chart with words from the Word Bank.

for "Sad"	for "Surprised"	for "Excited"	for "Sorry" or "Embarrassed"
forlorn	amazed	delighted	humbled
melancholy	astounded	exhilarated	
1. _____	3. _____	4. _____	6. _____
2. _____		5. _____	7. _____

Vocabulary

Word Play

Directions: Use the clues to solve each riddle with a word from the Word Bank.

Word Bank

ashamed	dejected	guilty
astonished	enthusiastic	thrilled
	glum	

1. Name an antonym for **joyful** that rhymes with **thumb**.

   _____

2. Name an antonym for **disappointed** that rhymes with **chilled**.

   _____

3. Which word begins like **astronaut** and ends like **finished**?

   _____

4. Name an antonym for **proud** that ends like **blamed**.

   _____

5. Name an antonym for **negative** that ends like **fantastic**.

   _____

6. Which word begins like **delay** and ends with **ejected**?

   _____

7. My first syllable rhymes with **wilt**, and my second sounds like **tea**. I'm an antonym for *innocent*. Which word

   am I? _____

Write About Your Troubles and Give Some Advice

Directions: Work in pairs. Partner A plays the role of a person with a problem. Partner B pretends to be a newspaper writer who answers letters from troubled people. A writes a letter and B answers it. Use words from the Word Bank in your letters. For help, use the example below.

Dear Aunt Agony:

My brother goes around looking glum all the time, and I want to find out what's troubling him. I think he may be feeling guilty about his grades—he got all Cs this semester. Average grades are nothing to be ashamed of, but he seems pretty dejected about it. I'm worried about asking him what's wrong, because I got better grades than he did. What's your advice?

Signed,
Sister in Cincinnati, Ohio

Dear Cincinnati Sister:

I must say I'm thrilled to hear from a sister who cares so much about her brother's feelings. But I'm astonished that your parents haven't yet had a talk with your brother. Or have they? If I were you, I'd ask them. Your brother may not be very enthusiastic about sharing his feelings with you, but that doesn't mean you can't share your concerns about him with your parents.

Yours truly,
Aunt Agony

Just the Opposite

Word Bank			
cowardly	cramped	generous	gobble
nibble	spacious	stingy	valiant

Getting to Know New Words

Directions: Read each sentence. Then choose the best word or phrase to replace the underlined word(s). Circle the letter next to your choice.

1. The <u>cowardly</u> boy did not defend his friend against the bullies.
   - a. brave
   - b. fearful
   - c. angry
   - d. unfriendly

2. There was only enough space for a bed and dresser in the <u>cramped room</u>.
   - a. room without enough space
   - b. room with too many windows
   - c. messy room
   - d. shared room

3. My <u>generous</u> grandparents buy me many presents.
   - a. careless
   - b. unselfish
   - c. gentle
   - d. glum

4. Our dog tends to <u>gobble</u> her breakfast—within seconds it's gone!
   - a. eat in large, quick bites
   - b. eat politely in tiny bites
   - c. waste
   - d. hide

5. I watched a mouse take a cracker crumb in its paws and <u>nibble on it</u>.
   - a. take large, quick bites of it
   - b. take tiny bites of it
   - c. chew on it without swallowing
   - d. tear it into tiny pieces

6. The Boyntons' new home is so <u>spacious</u> that they can host big parties.
   - a. roomy
   - b. beautiful
   - c. comfortable
   - d. close by

7. The story character was so <u>stingy</u> that he hated to spend even a penny of his wealth.
   - a. strange
   - b. cheap
   - c. stupid
   - d. angry

8. The <u>valiant</u> hero rode off to fight the dragon and rescue the princess.
   - a. joyful
   - b. loving
   - c. scared
   - d. brave

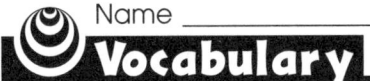
Vocabulary Practice

Directions: Find the antonym pairs. For each word from the Word Bank, write one with the opposite meaning.

1. valiant_____

2. nibble _____

3. spacious_____

4. stingy_____

Word Bank

cowardly

cramped

generous

gobble

nibble

spacious

stingy

valiant

Extra Practice

Directions: Use the words you paired in items 1–4 above.
Complete each two sentences by writing an antonym pair.

5. It's _____ to defend your little brother
   against bullies. But it's not _____ to ask a
   teacher or the principal for help.

6. Don't be so _____ with your money! Look
   how _____ Annie is—she gave ten dollars
   of her savings to help feed homeless people.

7. In our old house, my brother and I shared a
   _____ bedroom about ten feet square.
   But our new house is so _____ that each
   of us has our own room.

8. It's impolite to
   _____ your
   food as if you hadn't eaten in a
   week. But neither should you
   _____ your
   bread like a squirrel eating a nut!

Word Play

Directions: Read the paragraph below. Then complete the chart with words from the Word Bank.

About word connotations: Besides their exact meanings, words may have bad or good connotations. For example, *skinny* and *slender* both mean "thin." However, *skinny* has bad connotations, or suggests something negative. And *slender* has good connotations, or suggests something positive.

Word Bank	
cowardly	nibble
cramped	spacious
generous	stingy
gobble	valiant

Words About...	Words with Good Connotations	Words with Bad Connotations
being thin	slender	skinny
eating	1. _____	2. _____
soldiers in battle	merciful 3. _____	bloodthirsty 4. _____
saving money	thrifty	5. _____
spending money	6. _____	wasteful
large spaces	airy, roomy 7. _____	empty, echoing
small spaces	cozy, snug	crowded 8. _____

Write a Fairytale

Directions: Use a few words from the Word Bank to write the first two or three paragraphs of a fairytale. Use the example to help you. If you have time, finish your tale.

The Generous Old Woman and the Stingy Gentleman

Once upon a time there was a kind, generous old woman. She lived in a cramped little cottage and had little money, but she shared what she had with people in need. She figured she could always get along somehow or other.

In the same kingdom, there lived a rich but stingy gentleman. His house was spacious but almost empty, for he was too cheap to buy much furniture. At mealtime he drank water and nibbled on crusts of bread as if he were a beggar. But his basement was crammed with sacks of gold.

Vocabulary

body- and health-related nouns and verbs; multiple-meaning words

At the Doctor's Office

Word Bank			
examine	gash	intestines	limbs
medicine	remedy	skeleton	

Getting to Know New Words

Directions: Read each sentence. Then choose the best word or phrase to replace the underlined word(s). Circle the letter next to your choice.

1. My doctor uses a special light to <u>examine</u> my throat.
   - a. warm
   - b. heal
   - c. look carefully at
   - d. remove germs from

2. When I fell I slashed my leg on a sharp rock, so now I have <u>a gash</u>.
   - a. a scrape
   - b. a terrible sunburn
   - c. an itchy rash
   - d. a long, deep cut

3. When it is partly digested, food goes from your stomach to your <u>intestines</u>.
   - a. long tubes curled in your belly
   - b. body parts that help you breathe
   - c. kidneys and liver
   - d. heart and lungs

4. I've never broken any <u>limbs</u>, but my sister has broken an arm and a leg.
   - a. fingernails
   - b. school rules
   - c. fingers and toes
   - d. arms and legs

5. Mom worried that the tree would damage our roof, so she sawed off some of its <u>limbs</u>.
   - a. thick branches
   - b. twigs and leaves
   - c. leaves
   - d. fruit

6. Drink this <u>medicine</u> to help you stop coughing.
   - a. drug
   - b. soup
   - c. juice
   - d. tea

7. Baking soda mixed with a little water is a good <u>remedy for bee stings</u>.
   - a. mixture for preventing bee stings
   - b. mixture for healing bee stings
   - c. baking mixture with honey
   - d. mixture for attracting bees

8. Your <u>skeleton supports</u> your whole body.
   - a. bones hold up
   - b. muscles hold up
   - c. blood holds energy for
   - d. skull holds the brain for

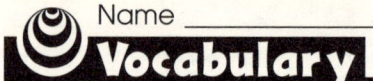
Vocabulary Practice

Directions: Write the word from the Word Bank that best completes each group or sentence.

1. prescription, pills, cough syrup, _____

2. check out, look closely at, _____

3. skull, bones, Halloween, _____

4. arms, legs, branches, _____

5. wound, cut, deep, _____

6. stomach, belly, digestion, _____

7. Ginger ale—in tiny sips—is one _____
   for an upset stomach.

Word Bank

examine	gash	intestines	limbs
medicine	remedy	skeleton	

Extra Practice

Directions: Choose the best way to complete each sentence or answer each question. Write the correct letter on the line.

1. What is a **skeleton's** head called? _____   a. sore

2. Who has strong, muscular **limbs**? _____   b. a doctor

3. Who prescribes **medicine** for her patients? _____   c. lotion

4. What is one **remedy** for dry skin? _____   d. a skull

5. Your **intestines** are long tubes inside _____.   e. stitching it up

6. Dr. Chang treated his patient's **gash** by _____.   f. an athlete

7. A doctor might **examine** your throat if it feels _____.   g. your belly

⊙ Vocabulary

Word Play

Directions: Read the information on analogies. Then write a word from the Word Bank on each blank line. Use the clues to help you.

Analogies usually have two pairs of words, like this:

carrot is to vegetable as orange is to _____.

In the example above, your job is to find the missing word that goes with *orange*. First you will need to figure out how the first pair of words relate to each other. Try to form a sentence that explains how *carrot* and *vegetable* are related. For example: *A carrot is one kind of vegetable.* Then you can plug in your answer: *An orange is one kind of what? Oh, of course—an orange is one kind of fruit!*

1. Lungs are to breathing as _____ are to digesting.	**Word Bank**
2. Supermarket is to groceries as drugstore is to _____.	examine
3. Muscles are to movement as _____ is to support.	gash
4. Fix is to repair as check out is to _____.	intestines
5. Hot is to burn as sharp is to _____.	limbs
6. Heart is to internal organs as arm is to _____.	medicine
7. Smiling is to enjoyment as _____ is to illness.	remedy
	skeleton

Write a Conversation Between a Nurse and a Doctor

Directions: Using a few words from the Word Bank, write a short conversation that a nurse and doctor might have in a medical office. Use the example to help you.

A Conversation in Dr. Boynton's Office

"Doctor, Mr. Pannocky is here again. He wants you to examine his sore ankle."

"Did he break it or twist it? Is it achy and puffy?"

"No, I believe he was bitten by a ferocious mosquito. He wants to know if we can recommend a good remedy for redness and unbearable itching."

"Tell him to go to the drugstore and buy some anti-itch medicine, for goodness sake!"

"What's the matter, Doctor? You look pale and sweaty."

"I shouldn't have had spicy food for dinner last night. I've got these terrible gas pains in my intestines."

"Why don't you go lie down in the examination room for a while? I'll tell your patients to expect a short delay."

Word Families

Word Bank			
befriended	checkout	checkup	friendless
homer	homesickness	homey	rechecking

Getting to Know New Words

Directions: Read each sentence. Then choose the best word or phrase to replace the underlined word(s). Circle the letter next to your choice.

1. Sierra <u>befriended</u> Eliza, a new girl in class, because Eliza seemed smart and funny.
   a. felt sorry for
   b. offered her friendship to
   c. introduced her friends to
   d. felt jealous of

2. Dad took our groceries to the <u>checkout</u> and paid for them.
   a. grocery cart
   b. store owner
   c. payment counter
   d. produce counter

3. When he went in for his last medical <u>checkup</u>, Pablo weighed seventy-five pounds.
   a. scale
   b. examination
   c. doctor
   d. search

4. If you keep quarreling with your friends, you may end up <u>friendless</u>.
   a. angering your friends
   b. hurting friends' feelings
   c. with only a few friends
   d. without any friends

5. Barry Bonds of the San Francisco Giants hit seventy-three <u>homers</u> in 2001.
   a. home runs
   b. foul balls
   c. baseballs
   d. home games

6. <u>Homesickness</u> is a common problem among the younger kids at summer camp.
   a. wishing they lived at camp
   b. having no friends at camp
   c. missing their homes
   d. disliking camp food

7. You can use colorful curtains and rugs to make a new apartment look <u>homey</u>.
   a. homelike
   b. stylish
   c. cluttered
   d. colorful

8. I kept <u>rechecking</u> to make sure that my little brother was still behind me.
   a. hurrying
   b. looking again
   c. walking
   d. slowing down

Vocabulary

Vocabulary Practice

Directions: Complete the chart by writing each word from the Word Bank in the correct column.

Word Bank

befriended	checkup	homer
checkout	friendless	homesickness
homey	rechecking	

Word Families

check	friend	home
checked	friendly	homework
double check	friendship	homemade
spot check	girlfriend	6. _____
1. _____	4. _____	7. _____
2. _____	5. _____	8. _____
3. _____		

Extra Practice

Directions: Choose the best way to complete each sentence or answer each question. Write the correct letter on the line.

1. **Friendless** people probably feel _____.

2. Where do people take their pets for **checkups**? _____

3. Who works behind a **checkout** counter? _____

4. When might someone suffer from **homesickness**? _____

5. Someone who keeps **rechecking** the time probably feels

   _____.

6. When a batter hits a **homer**, how many runs does

   her team score? _____

7. In a **homey** room, most people would feel _____.

8. Danny and David **befriended** each other and became

   _____.

a. to the vet

b. best buddies

c. lonely

d. one or more

e. while traveling

f. a cashier

g. anxious

h. comfortable

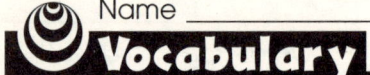 **Vocabulary**

Word Play

Directions: Use the clues to solve each riddle with a word from the Word Bank.

> **Word Bank**
>
> befriended   checkup   homer
>
> checkout   friendless   homesickness
>
> homey   rechecking

1. Which word begins like **bewildered** and ends with **ended**? _____

2. Name a synonym for **cozy** that rhymes with **foamy**. _____

3. Which word begins like **checkered** and ends like **holdup**? _____

4. Which word begins like **recharge** and ends like **pecking**? _____

5. Which word begins like **homework** and ends like **summer**? _____

6. Which word begins like **checkmark** and ends like **knockout**? _____

7. Name an antonym for **popular** that ends with **endless**. _____

8. My first syllable rhymes with **comb**. My second and third syllables rhyme with **thickness**. Which word am I? _____

Write a Poem Using Related Words

Directions: Choose one of the following words: *art, back, black, hard, soft, white,* or *wood.* Next, use the word you chose to make a list of related words—words in the same family. Use your list to write a poem that does not rhyme, as in the example:

Soft Beige Fur with White Spots

Treading softly

in soft morning light,

my heart softens

to see, nestled in moss

softer than cotton,

a soft-eyed fawn.

◉ Vocabulary

English Words from French and Spanish

Word Bank			
ballet	banquet	boulevard	café
canyon	patio	plaza	ranch

Note on English words from other languages: English includes many words from other languages. *Bagel* is a Yiddish word, *kimono* is Japanese, and the word *pajamas* comes from Persian, a language spoken in the Middle East. Can you figure out which four words in the Word Bank are French and which four come from Spanish?

Getting to Know New Words

Directions: Read each sentence. Then choose the best word or phrase to replace the underlined word(s). Circle the letter next to your choice.

1. In ballet class, Taylor learned to take graceful leaps across the floor.
   a. art
   b. volleyball
   c. basketball
   d. dance

2. At the banquet honoring our coach, we had vegetable pasta.
   a. performance
   b. fancy dinner
   c. breakfast
   d. costume party

3. The restaurant is located on a wide boulevard in Westwood.
   a. circle
   b. park
   c. street
   d. river

4. We ate breakfast at a little café near the highway.
   a. restaurant
   b. park
   c. picnic table
   d. old house

5. A river formed this deep canyon over thousands of years.
   a. pit
   b. secret
   c. valley with steep sides
   d. low, flat, grassy plain

6. The Pines have a barbecue grill and a picnic table out on their patio.
   a. outdoor paved area
   b. kitchen floor
   c. living room floor
   d. private beach

7. Most New Mexican communities have a central plaza in town.
   a. library
   b. police department
   c. public square
   d. heating company

8. My uncle raises horses, sheep, and cattle on his ranch.
   a. vacations and weekends
   b. large farm for growing crops
   c. small farm for producing milk
   d. large farm for raising animals

🎯 Vocabulary

Vocabulary Practice

Directions: Write the word from the Word Bank that best completes each group.

1. valley, cliff, rocky,

   _____

2. formal, dinner, wedding,

   _____

3. stage, ballerina, dance,

   _____

4. restaurant, coffee shop, _____

5. drive, street, avenue, _____

6. terrace, backyard, outdoor, _____

7. square, shopping center, _____

8. horses, cattle, range, _____

Word Bank

ballet

banquet

boulevard

café

canyon

patio

plaza

ranch

Extra Practice

Directions: Choose the best way to answer each question. Write the correct letter on the line.

1. Whom might you find in a **canyon**? _____

2. Who might work in a **café**? _____

3. Who might host a **banquet**? _____

4. Where can you see people practicing **ballet**? _____

5. What is a synonym for **boulevard**? _____

6. What might you find on a **patio**? _____

7. Where might you find a **plaza**? _____

8. Who might work on a **ranch**? _____

a. avenue

b. a waitress

c. a hiker

d. outdoor furniture

e. a bride's family

f. in the center of town

g. in a dance studio

h. a cowboy

 **Vocabulary**

Word Play

Directions: Write a word from the Word Bank on each blank line. Use the example to help you.

Word Bank		
ballet	boulevard	canyon
banquet	café	patio
plaza	ranch	

Example: <u>Supermarket</u> is to <u>groceries</u> as <u>drugstore</u> is to _____.

Think: At a supermarket, you buy groceries. At a drugstore, you buy . . . what? Oh, of course: <u>Supermarket</u> is to <u>groceries</u> as <u>drugstore</u> is to <u>medicine</u>.

1. <u>Dining room</u> is to <u>indoors</u> as _____ is to <u>outdoors</u>.

2. <u>Gown</u> is to <u>dress</u> as _____ is to <u>dinner</u>.

3. <u>Creek</u> is to <u>stream</u> as <u>street</u> is to _____.

4. <u>Collage</u> is to <u>artwork</u> as _____ is to <u>dance</u>.

5. <u>High</u> is to <u>mountain</u> as <u>steep</u> is to _____.

6. <u>Vegetables</u> are to <u>garden</u> as <u>horses</u> are to _____.

7. <u>Clerk</u> is to <u>store</u> as <u>waitress</u> is to _____.

8. <u>Home</u> is to <u>private</u> as _____ is to <u>public</u>.

Write a Love Letter

Directions: Using a few words from the Word Bank, write a love note that a silly character might write. Use the example to help you.

My Dearest Loveliest Darling:

When I first set eyes on you in the town <u>plaza</u> last Thursday, I fell deeply, hopelessly in love! Your beauty was a <u>banquet</u> for my hungry eyes! Please accept these roses—their color reminds me of your rose-red lips. I beg you to meet me at that little <u>café</u> on Belleview <u>Boulevard</u> at 5 P.M. It has a romantic outdoor <u>patio</u> where we can gaze into each other's eyes as we eat ham and cheese sandwiches.

Yours forever and ever and ever and ever and ever and ever,
Jean-Pierre Pomplemousse

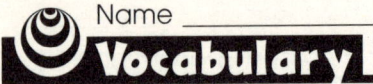

Vocabulary

Moving Around

Word Bank			
bustled	clung	collapse	demolished
discarded	eject	quivering	trudged

Getting to Know New Words

Directions: Read each sentence. Then choose the best word or phrase to replace the underlined word(s). Circle the letter next to your choice.

1. At Thanksgiving, three cooks <u>bustled</u> around the kitchen making a big dinner.
   a. sat lazily
   b. worked slowly
   c. moved angrily
   d. moved busily

2. On his first day of preschool, the little boy <u>clung</u> to his mom and cried.
   a. held tightly
   b. called
   c. laughed
   d. held loosely

3. An earthquake caused the bridge to <u>collapse</u>, but there were no cars on it.
   a. explode
   b. blow over
   c. fall down
   d. melt

4. Workers <u>demolished</u> the unsafe building and built a new one in its place.
   a. tore down
   b. repaired
   c. sanded and polished
   d. cleaned and painted

5. When a neighbor <u>discarded</u> her raggedy old sofa, I asked if I could have it for my clubhouse.
   a. sold
   b. bought
   c. threw out
   d. ripped open

6. Push that button to <u>eject the disk from</u> the computer.
   a. reach in and pull the disk from
   b. make the disk pop out of
   c. unglue the disk from
   d. untangle the disk from

7. During a thunderstorm, my dog hides under my desk, <u>quivering</u> with fear.
   a. scratching
   b. screaming
   c. snoring
   d. shaking

8. When the war was over, the exhausted soldiers <u>trudged</u> home in worn-out boots.
   a. walked tiredly
   b. flew
   c. took the bus
   d. jogged happily

Vocabulary Practice

Directions: Write the word from the Word Bank that best completes each sentence or group.

1. shoot out, pop out, _____

2. clutched, hugged, hung on,

   _____

3. recycled, threw out, cast off,

   _____

4. plodded, slogged, stumbled,_____

5. hurried, whisked, flitted, _____

6. destroyed, ruined, wrecked,_____

7. cave in, crumple, fall down,_____

8. shivering, shaking, trembling, _____

Word Bank
bustled
clung
collapse
demolished
discarded
eject
quivering
trudged

Extra Practice

Directions: Choose the best way to complete each sentence or answer each question. Write the correct letter on the line.

1. What can you do with **discarded** cans? _____

2. What can you **eject** from a VCR? _____

3. The rabbit's nose was **quivering** because it was _____.

4. A building that is about to **collapse** is probably _____.

5. Mom **bustled** around the house because she was _____.

6. The baby monkey **clung** to its mother so it wouldn't _____.

7. The hikers who **trudged** along the trail were probably _____.

8. You might see a **demolished** town following _____.

a. smelling the air

b. tired

c. very old

d. a videocassette

e. a war

f. busy

g. Recycle them.

h. fall

Vocabulary

Word Play

Directions: Use the clues to complete the crossword puzzle with words from the Word Bank.

Down

1. Fall down
2. Shivering
5. Thrown out
6. Pop out
7. Held tightly
9. I'm stuck—I can't _____.

Across

3. Grabbed
4. Destroyed
8. Walked tiredly
9. Moved quickly

Write a Chant or Cheer

Directions: Choose words from the Word Bank to write a marching chant or a cheer that fans might yell at a sports event. It is fine to change verb tenses if you need to. For instance, you might change *trudged* to *trudge* or *collapse* to *collapsing* as in the example:

A Marching Chant

We're weary but
We're cheery as
We trudge along the road!
We plod along,
We sing this song,
We carry a heavy load!
Collapsing's not allowed because
We know that once we stop,
We'll never budge again and so
We'll march until we drop!

Word Bank

bustled
clung
collapse
demolished
discarded
eject
quivering
trudged
budge
snatched

Vocabulary

Word Roots

Word Bank			
alphabetized	duet	duo	multicolored
multitude	pedal	sole	solo

Getting to Know New Words

Directions: Read each sentence. Then choose the best word or phrase to replace the underlined word(s). Circle the letter next to your choice.

1. In a dictionary, word entries are <u>alphabetized</u>.
   a. filled with definitions
   b. in ABC order
   c. in numerical order
   d. usually very short

2. Shelby and her sister sang a <u>duet</u> in the talent show.
   a. song sung by one person
   b. song sung by two people
   c. sorrowful song
   d. funny song

3. The two Dunn sisters decided to call their singing team "The Well Dunn <u>Duo</u>."
   a. threesome
   b. twosome
   c. singers
   d. family

4. Jack loved to gaze at the <u>multicolored</u> jellybeans in the candy store window.
   a. red, white, and blue
   b. neon green and shocking pink
   c. speckled
   d. many-colored

5. <u>A multitude of</u> cheering sports fans filled the stadium.
   a. a large number of
   b. loud, happy
   c. about thirty
   d. exactly one hundred

6. My little brother can <u>pedal his bike</u> on his own, but he still needs training wheels.
   a. clean and polish his bike
   b. change gears on his bike
   c. make his bike go by pushing on the foot pieces
   d. make his bike stop by squeezing the handbrakes

7. Long ago this was a farming community, but today ours is <u>the sole remaining farm.</u>
   a. the only farm left
   b. one of only two farms
   c. one of only a few farms
   d. the largest farm left

8. At the concert we each played a <u>solo</u>, and then we all played a song together.
   a. song for a large orchestra
   b. religious song
   c. funny song
   d. song for one musician

Vocabulary

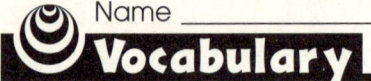

Vocabulary Practice

Directions: Complete the chart by writing each word from the Word Bank in the correct column. Before you start, read the note below.

Greek and Latin word roots: All of the words in this lesson have family ties with Latin or Greek. Both are ancient languages. One of the words from the Word Bank includes *alpha*, the Greek word for the letter *A*. Others come from Latin words meaning "alone," "two," "many," and "foot."

"Foot"	"Alone"	"Two"	"The Letter A"	"Many"
pedicure	solitary	duplex apartment	alphabet	multitalented
				multiply
1. _____	2. _____	4. _____	6. _____	7. _____
	3. _____	5. _____		8. _____

Word Bank

alphabetized	duo	multitude
duet	multicolored	pedal
	sole	solo

Extra Practice

Directions: Choose the best way to complete each sentence or answer each question. Write the correct letter on the line.

1. What is a dance **duo**? _____

2. What has four **pedals**? _____

3. How many honeybees are there in a **multitude**? _____

4. Who might play a **solo**? _____

5. Name something that's **multicolored**. _____

6. Who might play a **duet**? _____

7. Usually, students' last names are **alphabetized** for _____.

8. If you're the **sole** remaining person at the table, you're sitting _____.

a. a large number

b. a rainbow

c. roll call

d. all by yourself

e. two dancers

f. two piano players

g. one drummer

h. a bicycle built for two

◎ Vocabulary

Word Play

Directions: Write a word from the Word Bank on each blank line. Use the example to help you.

Word Bank		
alphabetized	duo	multitude
duet	multicolored	pedal
sole		solo

Lungs are to breathing as _____ are to digesting.

Think: I use my lungs for breathing. I use my "blank" for digesting. What body parts do I use for digesting food? Oh, yes—Lungs are to breathing as intestines are to digesting.

1. White is to snow as _____ is to rainbow.

2. Main is to major as only is to _____.

3. Trio is to three as _____ is to two.

4. Numerically ordered is to 1, 2, 3 as _____ is to A, B, C.

5. Skate is to skateboard as _____ is to bicycle.

6. Four is to a few as thousands are to a _____.

7. _____ is to song for one as _____ is to song for two.

Write a Travelogue

Directions: A travelogue is a true story about a trip that the writer took. Think of a place where you've been or place where you would love to go. Using a few words from the Word Bank, write a short travelogue about that place. Use the example to help you.

San Francisco: A Travelogue

Here I am on the streets of San Francisco. I watch a brave, strong bicyclist pedal up California Street, which is very, very steep. Is San Francisco's the sole remaining cable car system in the U.S.A.? If not, it's one of the few. I board a shiny wooden car and hang on tight. The conductor plays a Clang! Clang! Clang! solo on the warning bell that tells drivers and people on the street to keep out the way. Up, up, up we climb and then . . . down, down, down we plummet. This must be the hilliest city in the world!

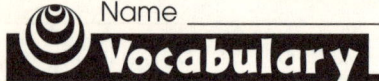
Review

Directions: Read the story. Then choose the best answer to each question about an underlined word. Circle the letter next to your answer.

Home with a Cold

"Basically, Miranda is a very healthy girl," Dr. Boynton told my mom when I went in for a <u>checkup</u> recently. But last winter I caught a terrible cold.

It was February, and the ground was still covered with snow from our latest <u>blizzard</u>. I <u>trudged</u> home from school feeling tired but otherwise okay. It wasn't until later in the evening that I began to suspect that I was sick. Colds are about the most common illness there is, so we can all recognize when we're getting a cold. Here's what aroused my suspicion: I wasn't just tired, I was <u>exhausted</u>. Plus, when I tried to sing my usual <u>solo</u> in the shower, my throat hurt.

Dad kept <u>rechecking</u> my temperature, though he said I didn't have a very high fever. He gave me a spoonful of a children's cold <u>remedy</u> called PediaCoddle. It's a sticky, red medicine that tastes like raspberries and smells like an <u>evergreen</u> tree. It made me so <u>drowsy</u> that I forgot to worry about the math test I was supposed to take the next day. Usually I try to <u>coax</u> my parents to let me stay up past my bedtime. But that night, all I wanted to do was <u>collapse</u> into bed.

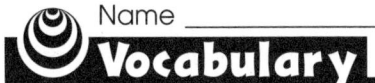
The next day I was so sick that I had to stay home from school. I felt glum about it, too—Barnacle Boulevard Elementary was having a talent show that day, and I was going to miss it. (However, I have to admit that I didn't feel at all dejected about missing my math test.)

I snoozed for most of the morning, and then Mom brought me some lunch in bed. I sat propped up on pillows and ate from a tray with a little vase of flowers on it. The flowers made me feel like a pampered princess with servants to wait on her. Unfortunately, I could only nibble on the toast that Mom served me. But the hot chicken broth and cool lime sherbet felt soothing as they slipped down my scratchy throat.

My cold was bad enough so that I couldn't budge from home for a whole week. By that time I was glad to get back to school—even though I did finally have to take that dreaded math test.

1. Miranda went in for a checkup so _____.
   a. Dr. Boynton could check her general health
   b. she could go back to school after a bad cold
   c. Dr. Boynton could check her math skills
   d. Dr. Boynton could give her a cold remedy

2. A blizzard is a _____.
   a. summer thunderstorm
   b. winter snowstorm
   c. hurricane
   d. hailstorm

3. A synonym for trudged is _____.
   a. collapsed
   b. sneezed
   c. scurried
   d. plodded

4. Complete this analogy: Tired is to exhausted as pretty is to _____.
   a. ugly
   b. beautiful
   c. girl
   d. drowsy

5. Who sings a solo?
   a. one singer
   b. a singing duo
   c. a singing trio
   d. a violin

6. Why does Dad keep <u>rechecking</u> Miranda's temperature?
   a. to see if it is going up
   b. to make sure she won't miss school
   c. because he doesn't believe that she is sick
   d. to make her fever go down

7. A cold <u>remedy</u> helps people _____.
   a. prevent colds
   b. feel better
   c. warm up
   d. avoid making others sick too

8. One kind of <u>evergreen</u> is a _____.
   a. rosebush
   b. maple tree
   c. pine tree
   d. cherry tree

9. <u>Drowsy</u> means the opposite of _____.
   a. wide awake
   b. dizzy
   c. sleepy
   d. deadly serious

10. Synonyms for <u>coax</u> are _____.
    a. urge, persuade, convince
    b. order, command, direct
    c. whine, moan, whimper
    d. trick, fool, hoodwink

11. Antonyms for <u>glum</u> are _____.
    a. sad, unhappy, in a bad mood
    b. happy, in a good mood, cheerful
    c. quiet, calm, sleepy
    d. loose, soft, weak

12. When Miranda says she "wanted to <u>collapse</u> into bed," that means _____.
    a. she wanted to jump into bed
    b. she wanted to read in bed
    c. she wanted to fall into bed
    d. she wanted to retire

13. Barnacle <u>Boulevard</u> is _____.
    a. an elementary school
    b. a street with a school on it
    c. a middle school
    d. an island with a school on it

14. <u>Dejected</u> is an antonym for _____.
    a. glad
    b. glum
    c. sly
    d. surprised

15. Probably Miranda can only <u>nibble</u> on toast because _____.
    a. it hurts her throat
    b. she has an upset stomach
    c. she doesn't like butter
    d. she isn't hungry

Teacher Resources

Tips for Teaching Vocabulary

Read aloud to students. Discuss the selection before, during, and after reading. As you read, define unfamiliar words, using synonyms, short definitions, and/or examples. Help students connect new words and concepts with their prior knowledge and experiences.

Encourage students to read on their own. The more students read independently—in school and at home—the more new words they will learn. Students can keep reading journals that include lists of words they encounter in their reading. Encourage them to collect hundred-dollar words (long, fancy ones), words they want to use in their writing, and words whose sounds and spellings they like. Ask students to contribute interesting words they come across in their reading to a class Favorite Words list displayed on chart paper.

Preteach words in reading selections. You may wish to use prereading vocabulary activities provided by your basal reading program's teacher guide. When choosing your own list of words to preteach, focus on these word types:

- **key words** whose meanings students will need to know in order to understand the reading selection's central concepts;

- **useful words** that students are likely to read, hear, say, and write again;

- **difficult words** such as multiple-meaning words, homographs, homophones, and unfamiliar idiomatic expressions, all of which can be troublesome for English language learners.

Include vocabulary instruction in all subject areas. Work with students to develop word walls, charts, and lists of math words, science words, social studies words, and words related to the fine arts. See the examples below.

Math and Money Words	Science Words	Social Studies Words	Music Words	Art Words
afford	acorn	agriculture	chorus	alabaster
bargain	broccoli	backwoods	duet	cameo
calculate	atmosphere	blacksmith	fiddle	collage
exceed	marine	citizen	instrumental	craftsperson
livelihood	microscope	reign	opera	scarlet
wealthy	wilderness	treason	solo	sculpture

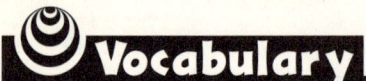

Teacher Resources

Enrichment Activities

Color Words: A Sorting Game

Write on separate slips of paper nouns and adjectives that name or describe colors (see the chart below). Place the slips in a bag and mix them up. Pairs or small groups of students can sort the words into Red Words, Orange Words, Yellow Words, and so on, using a dictionary as necessary.

Red	Orange	Yellow	Green	Blue
scarlet	tangerine	saffron	chartreuse	navy
maroon	vermilion	lemon	teal	turquoise
reddish	peach	mustard	forest____	cobalt ____
crimson	apricot	gold		

Pink	Purple	White	Black	Brown
magenta	violet	alabaster	ebony	mahogany
rosy	amethyst	snowy	inky	beige
shocking ____	lavender	milky	pitch____	fawn
	lilac	ivory		amber

Llamas, Pajamas, and Commas: A Word Categorizing Game

Player A says three words that are related in some way, without revealing their common bond. (Example: llamas, pajamas, and commas rhyme.) If Player B can guess the common bond, she says another word that fits (e.g., mamas). If she cannot guess it, she passes. Play continues until all players have guessed the common bond and no one can think of any more words that fit in the group. The last player to contribute a word gets to start the next group, but he may not use the same kind of common bond that Player A used. Possible game starters include

- scarlet, crimson, maroon (names for *red*)
- omelet, skillet, ballet (words ending with *-let*)
- knuckle, wrist, palm (hand parts)
- princess, principal, print (words beginning with *prin-*)
- purse, duffel bag, backpack (portable containers for people's possessions)

Teacher Resources

There's a Moth in My Grandmother

Write on the chalkboard a word that contains several smaller words. (For example, *grandmother* contains *grand, ran, and, an, moth, mother, other, he,* and *her.*) Have students work in pairs to write and pronounce as many words-within-a-word as they can. Ask them to underline words like *moth* that are pronounced differently from the way they sound as word parts.

Other long words that contain several shorter words include

- *bedraggled* (*be, bed, drag, rag, draggled, led*)
- *brotherhood* (*brother, other, he, her, hood*)
- *downhearted* (*do, down, own, hear, heart, ear, arf*)
- *fortunate* (*for, or, fort, tuna, Nate, at, ate*)
- *wholesome* (*whole, hole, holes, so, some, me*)

Students might use the words they find to write silly poems. For example:

Fortunate Nate
Back in 1948
when Nate was at
Fort Ord,
Nate thought he ate
a tuna plate
past its freshness date.
Fortunately,
the tuna
Nate ate
Wasn't bad
(though it wasn't great).

English Words from Other Languages: A Word Wall Activity

Help students brainstorm lists of American English words, including proper nouns, that come from French, Spanish, and other languages. Examples: *Los Angeles, San Francisco, California, patio, rodeo, ranch, tortilla, plaza* (Spanish); *Des Moines, café, restaurant, banquet, bouquet, omelet* (French); *kimono, sushi* (Japanese); *pizza, spaghetti, lasagna, pasta* (Italian); *wiener, sauerkraut* (German); *bagel, kibitz, schlep* (Yiddish); *pajamas* (Persian); and *bungalow* (Hindi). Divide a bulletin board into sections for different languages. Encourage students to write and illustrate context sentences for the words they contribute and post their work in the appropriate sections. As an extension activity, have students work in small groups to write a menu for an international restaurant, using the food words they collected on the word wall.

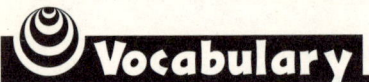

Teacher Resources

Before and After Word Puzzles

Write on the chalkboard widely used, simple words such as *table, chair, cat, book,* and *board*. Help students brainstorm lists of well-known phrases and compound words that contain them. (Examples: *tabletop, roundtable, table manners, coffee table; easy chair, armchair, chairperson, highchair; cat food, cat box, alley cat, catfish, cat burglar; workbook, phone book, bookcase, book cover, datebook; chalkboard, surfboard, ironing board, cardboard*.) Students can use these to create Before and After word puzzles such as

- *hot* _____ *house* (The solution is *dog—hotdog, doghouse*.)
- *video* _____ *worm* (The solution is *tape—videotape, tapeworm*.)

Building Words from Word Parts

Help students brainstorm lists of words with common prefixes and suffixes such as the following:

re- (again)	*dis-* (the opposite of; not)	*un-* (not)	*-less* (without)
readjust	discontinue	unable	flavorless
reawaken	dishonor	unconscious	homeless
rejoin	disinfect	unexpected	painless
restart	dislike	unfortunate	spotless
reuse	dismount	ungenerous	thoughtless
rewind	disprove	unsatisfied	worthless

-ful (full of)	*-some* (a group of a certain number)	*-some* (having a certain quality)
graceful	twosome	adventuresome
joyful	threesome	bothersome
sorrowful	foursome	troublesome
thoughtful		
vengeful		
wonderful		

Guide students to use their word groups to infer what the words' shared prefixes and suffixes mean. Then use a dictionary or the meanings listed above to check their guesses. Students may enjoy using prefixes, suffixes, and base words to invent silly words such as *cucumbersome, funless, unbrush,* and *discooperate*. Invite them to use their invented words in context sentences. Examples: I *dislike visiting Cousin Charlotte—we always have a <u>funless</u> time at her house. This salad is a little too <u>cucumbersome</u>.*

Teacher Resources

Antonym, Synonym, and Homophone Concentration

Write on separate index cards synonyms, antonyms, and homophones such as *vast/spacious, stern/severe, limber/flexible; exhaust/refresh, rare/common, reveal/conceal, seldom/frequently; woe/whoa, vein/vain, course/coarse, barren/baron, assistants/assistance* and *alter/altar*. Students can turn the cards face down on a large tabletop and use them to play Concentration. Tell them that they can pair words that sound the same (homophones), have similar meanings (synonyms), or have opposite meanings (antonyms). Later students can use their word pairs to write context sentences or jokes based on word play.

Dictionary Scavenger Hunt

Using the student dictionary available in your classroom, find words that may be unfamiliar to your students. Write several questions that students can answer by looking up dictionary entries. For example:

1. How is **ragweed** harmful to some people? (Some people are allergic to it. It makes them sneeze.)

2. Is a **feat** something to be ashamed of? What is a homophone for this word? (No, a feat is a courageous act. *Feat* and *feet* are homophones.)

3. The word **fax** is a shortened version of what word? How is a fax like an email? (*Fax* is short for *facsimile*, which means "copy." Faxes and emails are both messages that can be sent via telephone lines.)

4. Does the word **puma** have to do with: 1) cars; 2) carnivals; or 3) carnivores? (Carnivores—a puma is a large, meat-eating wild cat that lives in the Americas.)

5. What are two meanings for **kitty**? (a kitten or cat; money collected for a certain purpose)

Students can work individually or in pairs to find the answers. The first student or pair finished can use the dictionary to write a final bonus question for classmates.

Teacher Resources

Down with Boredom Board: A Word Wall Activity

Help students brainstorm a list of words and phrases that contain the "bore" sound spelled in a number of ways. Examples: *bore, boring, bored, boredom, board, chalkboard, bulletin board, boarded, boarding, room and board, skateboard, surfboard, ironing board, cutting board* and *boar.* Encourage them to write a context sentence for each word they contribute. Students can illustrate their sentences with drawings or magazine pictures and post them on a classroom bulletin board. They may also wish to include puns, jokes, or riddles based on homophone pairs such as bore/boar and bored/board. For example: **Q:** What did the pig say to her husband? **A:** You're such a boar!

You might use the activity as an opportunity to teach less familiar meanings for *bore: Some insects bore holes in wood; My grandparents bore great hardships.* You may also wish to teach less familiar meanings for *board: We board the bus at the corner; The school board voted to buy new uniforms for sports teams.*

Books on Vocabulary Instruction

Bear, Donald R., et al., *Words Their Way: Word Study for Phonics, Vocabulary, and Spelling Instruction* (Merrill Publishing, 1996)

Blachowicz, Camille, and Peter Fisher, *Teaching Vocabulary in All Classrooms* (Prentice Hall, 2001)

Nagy, William E., *Teaching Vocabulary to Improve Reading Comprehension* (International Reading Association, 1988)

Rasinski, Timothy V., ed., et al., *Teaching Word Recognition, Spelling, and Vocabulary: Strategies from the Reading Teacher* (International Reading Association, 2000)

Tompkins, Gail E., and Cathy L. Blanchfield, *Teaching Vocabulary: 50 Creative Strategies, Grades K-12* (Prentice Hall, 2003)

Evaluating student responses to writing activities: Responses will vary but should reflect understanding of list words' meanings. Also check for correct spelling, grammar, punctuation, and format, as well as creativity and vivid descriptions. Encourage students to use examples as format models and creative jumping-off spots. If they tend to copy, you may wish to present the activities without examples.

Our Five Senses 6–8

Getting to Know New Words
1. c
2. d
3. d
4. c
5. b
6. a
7. a
8. d

Vocabulary Practice
1. watermelon
2. greenery
3. odor
4. perfumed
5. hisses
6. beige
7. rumbled
8. slick

Extra Practice
1. d
2. g
3. c
4. f
5. e
6. a
7. b
8. h

Word Play
DOWN
1. beige
4. chilly
5. hisses
7. perfumed
10. odor

ACROSS
2. rumbled
3. applesauce
6. slick
8. greenery
9. watermelon

Dressing Up.......................9–11

Getting to Know New Words
1. a
2. a
3. b
4. c
5. b
6. d
7. a
8. c

Vocabulary Practice
1. sleeve
2. badge
3. wreath
4. shabby
5. lace
6. overalls
7. scarf

Extra Practice
1. c
2. e
3. a
4. b
5. g
6. f
7. d

Word Play
1. badge
2. crown
3. shabby
4. scarf
5. sleeve
6. overalls
7. lace
8. cotton
9. lace
10. wreath

Mystery word: dry cleaner

People You Meet 12–14

Getting to Know New Words
1. b
2. a
3. d
4. a
5. c
6. a
7. b
8. b

Vocabulary Practice
1. pupil
2. widow
3. veterinarian
4. astronaut
5. newcomer
6. relative
7. volunteer
8. astronomer

Extra Practice
1. e
2. a
3. h
4. d
5. b
6. c
7. f
8. g

Word Play
DOWN
1. tailor
3. veterinarian
4. bride
5. newcomer
8. astronaut

ACROSS
2. relative
6. widow
7. astronomer
9. pupil
10. volunteer

Right on Time!....................15–17

Getting to Know New Words
1. b
2. d
3. d
4. c
5. d
6. a
7. c
8. c

Vocabulary Practice
1. conclude
2. annual
3. ancient
4. mature
5. briefly
6. modern
7. future
8. seldom

Extra Practice
1. b
2. h
3. d
4. f
5. e
6. g
7. a
8. a

Word Play
1. conclude
2. annual
3. seldom
4. modern
5. ancient
6. future
7. briefly
8. mature

What Does That Stand For?.........18–20

Getting to Know New Words
1. d
2. a
3. b
4. b
5. a
6. c
7. a
8. d

Vocabulary Practice
1. g
2. d
3. f
4. a
5. e
6. h
7. b
8. c

Extra Practice
1. P.M., A.M.
2. CD, VCR
3. R.S.V.P., P.S.
4. U.S.A., www

Word Play
1. P.S.
2. VCR, CD
3. R.S.V.P., P.S.
4. www
5. A.M., P.M.
6. U.S.A.

High Tech....................21–23

Getting to Know New Words
1. d
2. a
3. b
4. b
5. c
6. a
7. d
8. a
9. c

Vocabulary Practice
1. PC
2. monitor
3. keyboard
4. mouse
5. software
6. Internet
7. Web site
8. Web address

Extra Practice
1. d
2. a
3. c
4. h
5. f
6. b
7. e
8. g

Word Play
1. printer
2. keyboard
3. PC
4. Internet
5. mouse
6. Web address
7. Web site
8. software
9. monitor

Can You Hear Me? 24–26

Getting to Know New Words
1. c
2. a
3. c
4. c
5. d
6. a
7. a
8. c

Vocabulary Practice
1. summoned
2. remarks
3. murmur
4. mumble
5. urged
6. bellowed
7. boasted
8. exclaimed

Extra Practice
1. e
2. a
3. g
4. h
5. f
6. b
7. d
8. c

Word Play
1. exclaimed
2. mumble
3. bellowed
4. urged
5. summoned
6. boasted
7. murmur
8. remarks

Tusks, Talons, and Tentacles.........27–29

Getting to Know New Words
1. c
2. a
3. c
4. a
5. b
6. a
7. c
8. c

Vocabulary Practice
1. jaguar
2. talons
3. burrow
4. tusks
5. galloped
6. scurry
7. tentacles
8. antlers

Extra Practice
1. c
2. f
3. a
4. h
5. b
6. e
7. d
8. g

Word Play
1. burrow
2. galloped; scurry
3. talons
4. antlers
5. tentacles; talons
6. jaguar
7. tusks

Let's Get Wet! 30–32

Getting to Know New Words
1. a
2. c
3. d
4. a
5. c
6. c
7. a
8. a

Vocabulary Practice
1. vessel
2. surf
3. evaporate
4. goggles
5. seep
6. blotted
7. moisten
8. squirt

Extra Practice
1. c
2. f
3. g
4. b
5. h
6. e
7. d
8. a

Word Play
1. broth
2. evaporate
3. squirt
4. moisten
5. vessel
6. blotted
7. goggles
8. surf
9. swamp
10. seep

Mystery word: rainstorms

Homophones 33–35

Getting to Know New Words
1. c
2. c
3. d
4. b
5. a
6. c
7. b
8. a

Vocabulary Practice
1. foul
2. allowed
3. ceiling
4. fowl
5. idle
6. aloud
7. idol
8. sealing

Extra Practice
1. idle; idol
2. sealing; ceiling
3. foul; fowl
4. aloud; allowed

Word Play
1. ceiling
2. foul
3. Allowed
4. sealing
5. fowl
6. idle
7. idol
8. aloud

Review **36–39**

1.	c	11.	d
2.	a	12.	a
3.	b	13.	c
4.	a	14.	c
5.	b	15.	a
6.	a	16.	c
7.	a	17.	b
8.	c	18.	a
9.	b	19.	b
10.	c	20.	c

Don't Be So Unfriendly! **40–42**

Getting to Know New Words

1.	b	5.	b
2.	a	6.	d
3.	b	7.	c
4.	d	8.	a

Vocabulary Practice

1.	suspicion	5.	quarreled
2.	condemned	6.	dispute
3.	contempt	7.	banish
4.	hostile	8.	coax

Extra Practice

1.	e	5.	g
2.	d	6.	f
3.	c	7.	a
4.	h	8.	b

Word Play

1.	accuse	6.	admit
2.	hostile	7.	condemned
3.	banish	8.	contempt
4.	dispute	9.	suspicion
5.	coax	10.	quarreled

Mystery word: conscience

The World Around Us **43–45**

Getting to Know New Words

1.	a	5.	d
2.	c	6.	c
3.	d	7.	a
4.	c	8.	b

Vocabulary Practice

1.	decayed	5.	crater
2.	fossil	6.	copper
3.	wilt	7.	blizzard
4.	evergreen	8.	equator

Extra Practice

1.	g	5.	d
2.	e	6.	f
3.	c	7.	b
4.	h	8.	a

Word Play

1.	decayed	5.	crater
2.	blizzard	6.	copper
3.	wilt	7.	evergreen
4.	fossil	8.	equator

Good Night, Sleep Tight! **46–48**

Getting to Know New Words

1.	c	5.	b
2.	d	6.	a
3.	b	7.	d
4.	c	8.	a

Vocabulary Practice

1.	moonbeam	5.	nightingale
2.	nestle	6.	drowsy
3.	exhausted	7.	arouse
4.	lullaby	8.	retire

Extra Practice

1.	d	5.	e
2.	c	6.	b
3.	a	7.	h
4.	g	8.	f

Word Play

DOWN

1.	moonbeam	6.	arouse
3.	nightingale	7.	twinkle
4.	lullaby		

ACROSS

2.	snooze	9.	retire
5.	exhausted	10.	nestle
8.	drowsy		

**How Do You Feel
About Synonyms?** **49–51**

Getting to Know New Words

1.	d	5.	a
2.	a	6.	b
3.	b	7.	c
4.	a		

Vocabulary Practice

1. enthusiastic
2. ashamed
3. dejected
4. ashamed; guilty
5. glum, dejected; or dejected, glum
6. enthusiastic; thrilled

Extra Practice

1-2. glum, dejected
3. astonished
4-5. enthusiastic, thrilled
6-7. ashamed, guilty

Word Play

1.	glum	5.	enthusiastic
2.	thrilled	6.	dejected
3.	astonished	7.	guilty
4.	ashamed		

Just the Opposite **52–54**

Getting to Know New Words

1.	b	5.	b
2.	a	6.	a
3.	b	7.	b
4.	a	8.	d

Vocabulary Practice

1.	cowardly	3.	cramped
2.	gobble	4.	generous

Extra Practice

5.	valiant; cowardly	7.	cramped; spacious
6.	stingy; generous	8.	gobble; nibble

Word Play

1.	nibble	5.	stingy
2.	gobble	6.	generous
3.	valiant	7.	spacious
4.	cowardly	8.	cramped

At the Doctor's Office **55–57**

Getting to Know New Words

1.	c	5.	a
2.	d	6.	a
3.	a	7.	b
4.	d	8.	a

Vocabulary Practice

1.	medicine	5.	gash
2.	examine	6.	intestines
3.	skeleton	7.	remedy
4.	limbs		

Extra Practice

1.	d	5.	g
2.	f	6.	e
3.	b	7.	a
4.	c		

Word Play

1.	intestines	5.	gash
2.	medicine or remedy	6.	limbs
3.	skeleton	7.	remedy or
4.	examine		medicine

Word Families **58–60**

Getting to Know New Words

1.	b	5.	a
2.	c	6.	c
3.	b	7.	a
4.	d	8.	b

Vocabulary Practice

1-3. checkout, checkup, rechecking
4-5. befriended, friendless
6-8. homer, homesickness, homey

Extra Practice

1.	c	5.	g
2.	a	6.	d
3.	f	7.	h
4.	e	8.	b

Word Play

1.	befriended	5.	homer
2.	homey	6.	checkout
3.	checkup	7.	friendless
4.	rechecking	8.	homesickness

**English Words from French
and Spanish** **61–63**

Getting to Know New Words

1.	d	5.	c
2.	b	6.	a
3.	c	7.	c
4.	a	8.	d

Vocabulary Practice

1.	canyon	5.	boulevard
2.	banquet	6.	patio
3.	ballet	7.	plaza
4.	café	8.	ranch

Extra Practice

1.	c	5.	a
2.	b	6.	d
3.	e	7.	f
4.	g	8.	h

Word Play

1.	patio	5.	canyon
2.	banquet	6.	ranch
3.	boulevard	7.	café
4.	ballet	8.	plaza

Moving Around **64–66**

Getting to Know New Words

1.	d	5.	c
2.	a	6.	b
3.	c	7.	d
4.	a	8.	a

Vocabulary Practice

1.	eject	5.	bustled
2.	clung	6.	demolished
3.	discarded	7.	collapse
4.	trudged	8.	quivering

Extra Practice

1.	g	5.	f
2.	d	6.	h
3.	a	7.	b
4.	c	8.	e

Word Play

DOWN

1.	collapse	6.	eject
2.	quivering	7.	clung
5.	discarded	9.	budge

ACROSS

3.	snatched	8.	trudged
4.	demolished	9.	bustled

Word Roots **67–69**

Getting to Know New Words

1.	b	5.	a
2.	b	6.	c
3.	b	7.	a
4.	d	8.	d

Vocabulary Practice

1. pedal
2-3. sole, solo
4-5. duet, duo
6. alphabetized
7-8. multicolored, multitude

Extra Practice

1.	e	5.	b
2.	h	6.	f
3.	a	7.	c
4.	g	8.	d

Word Play

1.	multicolored	6.	pedal
2.	sole	7.	multitude
3.	duo	8.	solo; duet
4.	alphabetized		

Review **70–73**

1.	a	9.	a
2.	b	10.	a
3.	d	11.	b
4.	b	12.	c
5.	a	13.	b
6.	a	14.	a
7.	b	15.	a
8.	c		